ALASKA
FOOTPRINTS

TWO TEACHERS FACE THE CHALLENGES
OF THE LAST FRONTIER

DARLENE L. LILIENKAMP

ARCHWAY
PUBLISHING

Archway Publishing books may be ordered
through booksellers or by contacting:

Archway Publishing
1663 Liberty Drive
Bloomington, IN 47403
www.archwaypublishing.com
844-669-3957

ISBN: 978-1-6657-5751-5 (sc)
ISBN: 978-1-6657-5752-2 (e)

Library of Congress Control Number: 2024904124

Print information available on the last page.

Archway Publishing rev. date: 02/26/2024

CONTENTS

ACKNOWLEDGEMENTS

Several people helped me to retell this couple's complicated and interesting story. Most of it comes from Allen Thompson's memory, supplemented by his wife, Connie Thompson. In addition, several of their friends including Sheila Howell (who was Sheila Weston during their early years in Alaska) and Connie Maxey helped fill in some details. Allen and Connie's oldest son, Bill, also provided many key details. Thank you to everyone for their contributions, especially Allen and Connie who were so gracious and generous in sharing their story and allowing me to be the one to write it down! What a glorious experience for me.

And thank you to my husband, Carl, my own Alaska adventure partner, who encouraged me every word of the way! His belief in me was a true encouragement and blessing. His memory will live in my heart and soul as long as I have breath.

And most importantly, I want to acknowledge God's power in all of this. After all, He is the one who created Alaska in all its wild and treacherous beauty and who made it possible for Carl and me to take our many trips there, seeing for ourselves the majesty of His creation in this place. Alaska captured my heart on our first trip up the Alaska Highway, touring as much as we could. We felt certain we would never be able to return, but return we did! It is also evident that God was with Allen and Connie as they lived (and survived) these stories!

As it turns out, our repeated trips we have been blessed to make to Alaska have made us feel like it is our second home. We treasure all the people we have met over the years and who have become precious friends.

To God be the glory!

Darlene Lilienkamp

December 2023

Allen and Darlene and a piece of baleen

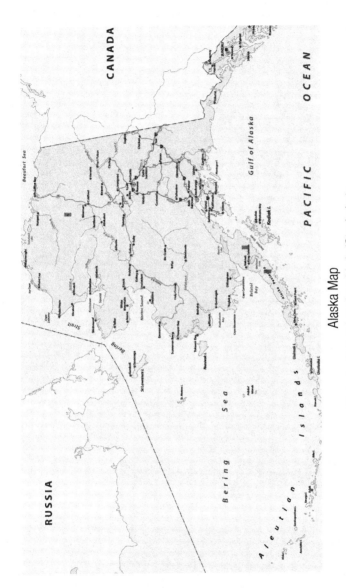

Alaska Map

Photo by Rainer Lesniewski via iStockphoto

CHAPTER 1

THE LURE OF ALASKA

An Alaska Introduction...

The mystical lure of Alaska! Many feel it–maybe even you! People plan and save for years to take that one trip of a lifetime, and some of those visitors decide after one visit to move to Alaska and make it their permanent home. Their hearts and imaginations belong to the almost endless wilderness.

Alaska has fourteen major mountain ranges containing ten of the eleven highest mountain peaks in the United States. Alaska's highways have numbers that most Alaskans do not use, preferring to refer to them by name: the Glenn, Old Glenn, Seward, Old Seward, Sterling, Taylor, Tok Cutoff, Richardson, Dalton, Parks, Top of the World, Steese, Edgerton, Klondike, and the famous and historic Alaska Highway. Only 25% of the communities in the state are accessible by these highways or on any road at all. When driving down one of these few highways, one can look out onto land that has probably never had any human footprints upon it.

According to the U.S. Geological Survey, a 2011 glacier study found that Alaska had roughly 27,000 glaciers. Only about one third of these have been named. These fascinating rivers of ice can be miles long and wide, thousands of feet thick, so heavy that they have carved out valleys and fjords. Yet tiny ice worms can live in the glacial ice. As more and more snow adds to the weight of the glacier, the ice becomes so dense that only the blue wavelength of light can escape, making the glacial ice a beautiful shade of blue. Glaciers have been and continue to be an essential geological feature of this state.

The fascinating history of Alaska includes the animals that lived there during the last ice age. Perhaps more than 10,000 years ago, a large portion of the land we call Alaska was covered with ice except for the land bridge that stretched from Siberia to the Yukon known as Beringia. This area was covered with the mammoth steppe, a rich grassland area and the home to giant beavers, Yukon horses, huge scimitar cats, steppe bison, giant short-faced bears, as well as other species that were isolated by the ice that surrounded them. Fossil remains of hairy elephant-like monsters, the wooly mammoth, are found sometimes with flesh still upon the bones. Their large ivory tusks are of great monetary value. The first humans also reached what is now Alaska over this land bridge. (https://www.beringia.com/exhibits/beringia)

Humans have lived in Alaska for thousands of years, using whatever natural resources they could find to survive, often in harsh environments. Many still live a subsistence lifestyle, and the hunters are the most important people in the village. Less than 20% of the Alaskan population is now made up of these Alaska Native groups. The names of the Native groups with their more than 20 distinct cultures and 300 dialects include the Athabaskan, Inupiat, Yup'ik, Cup'ik, Unangax, Alutiiq, Eyak, Haida, Tsimshian, Tlingit and more. Unless you have spent time in Alaska, these Native names are likely unfamiliar. (https://www.travelalaska.com/Things-To-Do/Alaska-Native-Culture)

Alaska Natives knew for centuries how valuable the furs of the animals in this cold climate were for tools, clothing, shelter, and boats. They used the meat, bones, and sinew, nothing going to waste, much like the lower-48 Natives used the bison for survival. As early as the mid-1600s, these luxurious furs became a desirable commodity for many besides the Natives. In the mid-1700s, the Russians essentially took control by trading with the Alaska natives for sea otter and other pelts, much desired by the Chinese aristocracy. The United States and Great Britain got involved when they noticed how profitable this could be. When animals were over hunted and demand dropped, the importance of the fur trade to these outsiders fell, but not before the Alaska Natives' lives were adversely affected by the diseases, alcohol, Native slavery and human trafficking that were ushered in with the fur trade. (source: www.https://encountersalaska.com/the-alaskan-fur-trade)

In more recent history, the discovery of gold in the 1800s opened an entirely new chapter in Alaska's history and brought a sudden influx of people from around the world who came and stayed, at least for a while, building towns that did not always survive. Then the discovery of oil on the North Slope in the 1900s, the far northern area of Alaska, brought immense wealth to people who only a few years earlier had no need for money. The change that this vast supply of money brought to those who lived in that area where nothing had changed for centuries is difficult to imagine.

Now the new gold rush is said to be tourism. People come to Alaska to enjoy the beauty of its mountains, glaciers, lakes and rivers, to try their skill at hunting and fishing, to brave the elements in mountain climbing, hiking, and kayaking. Tourists enjoy flight-seeing tours in one of the thousands of small airplanes that seem to be everywhere in Alaska. Summers are delightful times to be outdoors.

People from "outside" are often intimidated by the thought of Alaska winter. The longer nights and colder temperatures do not seem that inviting–until one witnesses the spectacular Northern Lights, the aurora borealis. Tourists come from around the world just to see that amazing natural phenomenon.

Alaskans seem to be on the move no matter what the weather is. Sled dogs, four-legged athletes, amaze spectators who come to watch short races or be impressed by the incredible obstacles presented by the Iditarod. Fur Rondy in Anchorage is billed as the nation's premiere winter festival. Its roots go back to the days when miners and trappers would come to Anchorage to sell and trade. Its "wild and wacky fun" represents the pioneering spirit so alive in Alaska, even to this day. The twelve-day festival attracts people from all over the world.

Even so, there are vast areas in the remote and inaccessible wild that have never felt the tread of a human footprint. It requires specific knowledge and skills to brave the elements that have claimed the lives of many who thought they were ready to tame this wilderness.

Meet the Thompsons...

On our many trips to this beautiful and fascinating state, my husband and I met several interesting people whose stories are worthy to be told, but this story is about Allen and Connie Thompson. My first clue that they had a story that needed to be told was their license plate. Not just any license plate, but a personalized Alaska license plate with the message "ICYBAY." There had to be a story–or two–or more–behind a couple that can legitimately display that message!

In 1961 Allen and Connie Thompson moved to Alaska at an opportune time when a person with ambition and creativity had so many possibilities right in front of them if they took time to notice and the spirit to attempt them. They were the type of people that Alaska needed–strong, adventurous, full of curiosity and ideas, willing to take risks and able to work back from failure, ready to be put to work in the Last Frontier. Teachers by profession and with love for their students in their hearts, they also ventured outside of this occupation to stretch themselves through other opportunities that carried them away from Alaska to other parts of the world. Not only did Alaska challenge them, but they also found unconventional things to attempt in Australia and Indonesia, giving them even more insights into those cultures and their own capabilities.

Allen, a self-described entrepreneur and educator, and Connie, a truly adventurous and loving support and accomplice, embarked on a lifetime of service from the day they met. They both were completely committed to their marriage vows which kept them together through many difficult transitions. Moving from Montana to near the Arctic to the tropics and back to Alaska required them to adjust to these diverse cultures quickly. In 1969, identity theft not only stole Allen's identity, but the thieves took all their carefully stored material possessions. In 1979, disaster struck a second time when they lost everything due to a bankruptcy. They were even left with no car of their own. The years that followed were filled with the efforts of working to pay off debts and lawyers.

When a friend of theirs heard about their devastating bankruptcy, she came to Anchorage to encourage them. Standing outside on the street during a beautiful winter snow, she told them, "Whenever two or more are gathered together, God will hear our prayer," and she prayed with them. That picture and those words have stayed with them since that night. It was only with the power of God in their lives and marriage that they were able to stick together through this and subsequent trials and come out stronger for it.

But that wasn't the end of it. Ten years after that, what little they managed to accumulate after the bankruptcy was destroyed in a fire at Wainwright, Alaska, when the high school burned. The prayer on that snowy day was a comfort and source of strength yet again.

When I asked them what they would have told their younger selves, Al replied, "Be careful!" Connie replied with the same attitude she went into their marriage with–"Never give up!" Although I'm not sure Al would have been willing to follow his own advice, it is safe to say that both of them did follow Connie's advice as they did not give up when devastating hardships seemed to block their way.

Although it was hard to see it back then, they both acknowledge that God had a plan, and they thank Him every day for getting them to the place they are today. Read on to share in this couple's unique story of how they left their footprints in many areas of the Last Frontier. They never gave up, even when disaster tried to stop them!

CHAPTER 2

ROOTS

Allen's Early Childhood

Allen was born in Havre, Montana, on January 22, 1939, and was adopted by Hazel and Bob Thompson when he was two years old. His early life was spent growing up in the rural phosphate mining town of Elliston, Montana, at an elevation of 5000 feet in the Rocky Mountains, just 25 miles from the state capital. In those days, no adopted children knew much about their birth families. He came to stay with the Thompsons when one of his mother's sisters, a social worker at the time, asked his adoptive mother, Hazel, to keep this young boy for a while until a home could be found for him. When the time came for Allen to go to a new home, Hazel said she wanted to keep him. His aunt was able to work it out that the Thompsons could keep this little one.

His parents had two biological children after they adopted Al, but Al feels he was never treated any differently than his siblings. Al felt that Bob and Hazel were truly his parents as they were the two people who raised him. He never pursued trying to find out anything about his birth parents or meet them.

When he was ten years old, Allen was playing near a deep hole to be used for an electric power pole. He threw a stick into the hole, and while trying to retrieve it, fell in head first, trapped upside down. His German shepherd, Pal, was a WWII veteran with his photo on display in the little town Al grew up in. Pal's military training as a communication dog kicked in when he saw the situation his beloved boy was in. The loyal dog ran home, tore a hole in the screen door, and got Al's mother's attention. His mom followed Pal back to where Al was trapped and unconscious and pulled him out of the hole. She slapped his face several times which had turned purple from lack of oxygen, and got him breathing again. This is just one of several traumatic events that Al has remembered for his entire life.

From Humble Hay to Gobs of Gold

His first job was at the tender age of 12 when his dad, dressed in humble bib overalls, looked him straight in the eye and told him he wasn't going to buy Al's clothes for him anymore. It was time for Al to get a job so he could buy his own clothes. His first job was at a hay ranch in Avon, Montana.

When he was 16, he worked in the evenings after school in a placer gold mine near Elliston, Montana. Placer mining finds eroded minerals in sand or gravel rather than in a vein of hard rock. The owner of the placer mine, Andy Van Francenen, was from France and knew very little English. He did not dress like an American, but usually wore French riding britches. Andy was an experienced miner who taught Al how to prospect for gold, pan for gold, and how to process the gold into little gold bars that were sold in the fall.

They started the mine in the New York Valley near Elliston. Andy taught Al to look for various rock formations, recognize potentially productive areas, and to sample minerals in likely areas, always looking for veins of gold that could be washed into the two sluice boxes they built. These sluice boxes had wood ripples in the bottom to catch the gold that was mixed with gravel. The heavier gold would settle out, captured by the ripples as the waste rock would wash out with the water.

After three years of working the placer mine, an unbelievable discovery appeared right before Al's eyes. He walked up to shut the dam off, cutting the water supply that controlled the hydraulic water gun used to wash the paydirt into the sluice box. As Al was walking down the edge of the work pit, he saw a stream of gold washing into the sluice box from a seam that was fifteen feet long by two feet wide–the mother lode! With great excitement, he ran to the cabin to get Andy. They cleaned up the gold, capturing it in a gold pan, pouring the gold into two buckets to be melted down into gold bars later. In about six hours, Andy netted $2.5

million of gold at $35 an ounce, a stunning moment in gold mining history.

Although Al didn't share in the wealth of this discovery, Andy always gave him a fair wage, paying him year-round, and treating him well. In the beginning when money was tight, Andy paid him with a quart of mercury which was valued at $300. Al never felt that he was underpaid, even after the mother lode discovery. Al feels that Andy played a large role in teaching him the value of work, the perfect person to work for as he taught Al the good work habits that he used for a lifetime. For this, Al is thankful.

Andy himself never had a chance to enjoy this wealth as one day within five or six months of this gold discovery, he slipped and fell on an icy step while on his way to work and died from his injuries. Al sprinkled some gold dust on his casket as he was being lowered into his grave in Helena, Montana. The mortician remarked that he had never seen that done before. Andy's wife took the wealth of the mine and shortly after Andy's death, moved back to the East coast.

The College Years

After Andy died, Al enrolled at Northern Montana College in Havre, Montana, with the goal of becoming a teacher. Maybe not so coincidentally, this was the fall of 1959, just a few months after Alaska gained statehood, a place that would be a major stage for much of Al's life.

Because he, like college students everywhere, was always short on money, he took two part-time jobs: one delivering milk to homes in glass bottles between 3:00 and 8:00 a.m., the other as an elementary school playground supervisor from noon to 1:00. He kept this schedule during his college years and was able to graduate with a teaching degree in 1961.

Death in a One-Room School

In March 1961, Allen had just graduated from Northern Montana College. He eagerly went off to his first teaching job in Joplin, Montana, a small rural wheat-farming community about 35 miles from the Canadian border. The remote one-room, grades 1-8 country school, had everything one could need, including an outhouse! Everything went well until one day a car drove up to the school house with its horn constantly blaring. At first Al ignored the disturbance, but it's hard to ignore an incessantly honking horn when one is trying to teach.

Finally, Al asked the children to remain in their seats while he checked on what the cause of the ruckus was. He opened the school door and saw someone slumped over the steering wheel, causing the horn to honk. He approached the car, opened the door, and an elderly gentleman breathlessly muttered, "I'm having a heart attack!" Al helped him into the school room, laid him on the floor with a pillow under his legs. The man started choking and died right in front of all the students in the classroom. Al called the PTA president who was able to identify the stranger as a local neighbor. Needless to say, teachers are not trained in how to deal with a situation such as this. Surprisingly, the children behaved well through it all, the body was removed, and the kids went out to recess and played. This was quite an introduction to classroom teaching. In no way did it deter him from pursuing a successful career in education that would go on to change the trajectory of many students' lives.

Al taught at this school only one semester before another major life-change occurred that all started back when he was a playground supervisor during his college days.

Connie's Early Childhood

Connie was born in 1936, right in the middle of the Great Depression. She grew up in eastern Montana on a large cattle ranch, fifty miles from the nearest town, Sidney, Montana. This homestead was settled by her father, Elmer Foss and his first wife Nena. Her dad was the son of a homesteader who had immigrated from Norway and claimed a homestead in Iowa. Connie's dad moved from that homestead in Iowa to claim his own in Montana in the early 1900s. He built a three-bedroom house that would eventually be populated with a large family.

Elmer Foss and Nena had four children. Several years after Nena died in childbirth, he married Dorothy. Connie was the fourth of eight children that Elmer and Dorothy had together—seven girls and then the youngest, a boy.

All of these children were born to their busy mom over a period of 10 years. Two of the older children from the first marriage lived in a bunkhouse and helped on the ranch, but all the rest shared the original house constructed when the homestead was claimed. Over the years, the house was expanded to accommodate this large family, and eventually had electricity and running water that replaced the outhouse.

While she was growing up during the Depression, food was scarce and some items, like sugar, were rationed. They learned at an early age to save. Connie remembers ration books for everything from sugar to shoes. The family never felt deprived as they had no idea what they did not have– everyone in the area lived like they did.

The children were taught and expected to work hard at a very young age. At the young age of six or seven, she was already expected to do her daily chores. These included milking cows and using a big 'separator' to separate the milk from the cream. They used this rich cream for cottage cheese, churning butter, and baking cookies and cakes. Every summer there were 100 chickens that required feeding in the morning and gathering eggs in the evening. In the fall, the whole family faced the task of butchering these chickens. Connie's hard-working mom had to cook three meals a day for 17-20 people, depending on how many extra mouths there were to feed when the harvest crew was working on the ranch.

By the age of 12, Connie and her siblings were also helping with the outdoor work of a cattle ranch. Driving the tractor, mowing and baling hay, then stacking the bales for the cattle for winter use was only part of her chores. And this could not be done only once in the summer! Cultivating corn was another summer chore. Winter did not grant a reprieve from hard physical labor. The hungry cattle in the pasture six miles from the house had to appreciate when Connie and her sister would, on even the coldest winter days, deliver a load of hay in the open hay wagon driven by her dad and pulled by two horses.

Connie's Montana home

Connie's School Days

Connie and her siblings were usually home schooled during their elementary school days. The country school with the teacherage next door was three miles from their house and often could not find a teacher. When there was a teacher at this small one-room school, the children would often ride their bicycles or horses to school. At its peak, the school had about nine students, their ages spread across all the grades, first through eighth.

When she was old enough to go to high school, the family bought a house in Sidney about eight blocks from the high school. This house, about 50 miles from where she grew up, had running water and electricity, but still no television. Until at least one of the girls was old enough to have a driver's license, her parents would drive Connie and her three oldest sisters the 50 miles to Sidney on Sunday night or Monday morning, depending on the weather. The girls would stay at the house all week, cooking and cleaning and taking care of themselves. They had all been taught from early on how to be responsible and work hard, so they all got along well with this arrangement. Their parents picked them up again on Friday night to spend the weekend at home.

When she graduated from high school, Connie had already known she wanted to be a teacher. She had decided this when she was only seven years old and never wavered from this plan. She attended St. Olaf College in Northfield, Minnesota, for her freshman year. Although she loved the school and the challenges it presented, she did not have the educational background needed for the challenges at this college. She wanted to continue her education and be closer to home and her sisters, so she transferred to Montana State in Bozeman.

The first time Connie was in a real elementary classroom was when she did her student teaching before college graduation.

Immediately after graduation from college in 1958 Connie was hired to teach first grade in another real classroom at the elementary school in Havre, Montana. And this is where the paths of two kids, both accustomed to hard work and taking on challenging tasks, crossed, for better or worse, in sickness and in health, for richer or poorer until death parts them, leaving their footprints side by side.

CHAPTER 3

THE JOINT ADVENTURES BEGIN

Allen and Connie Meet

Going back to his college days, the impetus for Al's two college-days jobs was, of course, to earn money, but the big draw to be lunchtime playground supervisor was not the $25 a month salary, but getting the hot lunch meal every day. Oh! -- and meeting that sweet first grade teacher through a blind date certainly became an added incentive to keep that job. In fact, this first-grade teacher became the main attraction.

When Connie first met Allen, she enjoyed talking with this kind and friendly guy who was also studying to become a teacher. Her best friend, also a teacher at the school in Havre, Norma Ricks, set Allen and Connie up on a blind double date with her and her husband who had been a college classmate of Allen's. It did not take long for Allen and Connie to develop a close friendship based on their many similar interests. It was a fun coincidence to discover that Connie's sister, Shirley, had been Allen's high school English teacher in Deer Lodge, Montana.

While dating, they often discussed the future and what they wanted, where they would live, and what they could do to be a part of that community. It was exciting to think about teaching together, a profession they both loved. They had decided that Alaska was the place to begin their teaching careers together. Alaska also appealed to Al because of all the hunting and fishing possibilities that Connie was willing to go along with, being accustomed to facing hard work and challenges since childhood.

After dating for three and a half years, Allen Thompson married Connie Foss on July 22, 1961, in Sidney, Montana. They had only been married four hours when they said goodbye to their parents, siblings and friends and headed North to Alaska. They had both applied and had good teaching jobs lined up there, Connie teaching first grade at Eielson Air Force Base near Fairbanks and Al teaching sixth grade at Fort Wainwright.

The Long and Bumpy "Highway"

Their honeymoon journey took them on the scenic route through Canada including a tour of Banff in their brand new expensive $2400 maroon and white 1961 Chevy truck and camper. A large segment of the journey required traveling on the Alaska Highway (Alcan), a road built hastily in 1942 for use by the military during World War II in order to service military outposts protecting the United States mainland from potential Japanese invasion after the bombing of Pearl Harbor.

The hastily built road was a challenge for the more than 11,000 soldiers in the Army Corps of Engineers who were assigned the task of its construction. Besides the military, at the height of construction 16,000 civilian contractors from the United States as well as Canada tackled this huge construction project. No one had experience in building in this relatively unexplored and uncharted area. Besides clearing dense forests and finding routes through and around challenging terrain, the road had to cross through swamps of decaying vegetation called muskeg. Permafrost was another daunting challenge for road construction. The surface of this permanently frozen ground would liquify with only a few degrees of warming only to refreeze when the cold returned. In summer, hordes of mosquitoes plagued the workers, and that fall was one of the most bitterly cold on record, with temperatures so cold that skin would freeze in seconds.

This 1500-mile-long highway was completed in about eight months, one of the greatest construction projects in American history. It was used exclusively by the military for a number of years, opening to civilian use in 1948 making it relatively new and still fairly primitive in 1961 when the Thompsons traveled it for the first time. The gravel "highway" had many curves and long stretches of bumps, dips and dramatic hills, making slow travel a necessity. Evidence of the road's construction was still visible when the Thompsons drove it—trees were still scattered and heaped together on the side of the road. Assorted pieces of abandoned construction equipment were just pushed off to the side of the road and left to rust and decay in the elements.

Knowing some of what was awaiting them for their trip up the Alcan, their vehicle was outfitted with plastic bubbles that covered the headlights and a large screen attached to the front bumper that reached just above the level of the hood to prevent gravel from chipping the paint, puncturing the radiator, and busting the windshield. Brand-new heavy-duty tires would withstand the brutality of the long 3000-mile journey, 1200 miles of this on gravel. Besides these practical accessories, they were sure to take enough cash along to buy large amounts of the twenty cents a gallon gas. Since this was their honeymoon, their truck was also outfitted with wedding decorations and reminders, a curiosity along the road wherever they stopped.

There being no alternate route where this remote road cuts through the wilderness, when they came to a washed-out bridge, a D-7 caterpillar backed up to their truck, hooked up to it with a chain, and towed it across the river, pulling them through the water. Finally, after a week of travel, they arrived at the Alaska border—and PAVEMENT. A relatively short drive (about 250 miles) from the Yukon/Alaska border north to Fairbanks brought them to the end of their long journey and the beginning of their Alaska adventure, planting their first Alaska footprints firmly in this place.

Fairbanks Arrival

They only had a couple of months to prepare for the six months of winter that was coming when they arrived in Fairbanks on August 17. Finding a place to live was their first priority, not an easy task in this frontier town with a population of just over 13,000. They finally found a place that had a small living room with a full-sized bed, a semi-comfortable chair, and a small chest of drawers complete with a TV on top. The kitchen was so small that three people could not fit into it at the same time, but they did have a small stove, a couple of cupboards, a small table and two small chairs. Keeping up with the "small" theme of their lodgings, the bathroom was also very small, but had all the necessities. They discovered that the brown paint on the bathroom walls had a practical purpose. It helped to cover up the iron-laden water stains that also turned their fingernails and toenails brown after a period of a few months.

They were making it just fine in these cramped quarters, and then a knock on the door made it a bit more challenging. Al's friend, Bob, had come to Fairbanks to work and needed a place to stay for a while. Of course, Alaska hospitality would not turn a friend in need away, so Bob stayed with them for three weeks until Al suggested Bob needed to find another place to live.

As is typical for the Fairbanks area, their first winter was brutal with at least one negative 72-degree day and the sun just peeking over the horizon for a short time every day. Add to that the freezing ice fog–tiny ice crystals–that formed from the moisture of the Chena River that runs right through town, beautiful but potentially dangerous. It can limit visibility and make driving treacherous as it coats the roadways. Early settlers called it the "white death" as they believed the ice crystals would settle in one's lungs and cause death.

At the end of the school term, they closed up the apartment and drove back down the Alcan Highway for a summer getaway and a visit to their Montana relatives before school resumed again in the fall. This was the second of what would become 17 trips on this glorious historic road during the many years they lived in Alaska.

CHAPTER 4

THE FAIRBANKS HOMESTEAD 1961-1964

Homesteading in Alaska

Homesteading began in the United States in 1862 when President Abraham Lincoln signed the 1862 Homestead Act. Over the next nearly 125 years, 270 million acres of land, most intended for family farms, was claimed in 30 states, about one tenth of all land in the United States.

Although President William McKinley signed legislation extending homesteading into the "Alaska District" on May 14, 1898, not many claims were made until 1912, after Alaska became a territory. Even then, most homesteads in Alaska were not filed until after World War II. When homestead laws were repealed elsewhere, Alaska was still open to homesteading for another ten years. The last day to file a homestead claim in Alaska was October 20, 1986.

Requirements to farm the land on a homestead claim were not practical in most areas of Alaska because of climate and the short growing season. In addition, there was limited opportunity to market a crop or get the expensive equipment and supplies needed to plant and harvest a crop.

Military veterans had special rights to obtain homesteads faster than normal homesteaders. Women and minorities could claim a homestead, and several did just that. Immigrants who wished to become citizens of the United States were also allowed to file for homesteads.

Homesteading was an important part of United States history, playing an important role in its expansion and development. The Thompsons were just one of the more than 1.6 million homesteaders during this important historic era of America, planting footprints on a previously unsettled parcel of land.

(Source: https://www.blm.gov/sites/default/files/documents/files/PublicRoom_Alaska_Homesteading_Brochure_2016.pdf)

Free Land

Shortly after arriving in Fairbanks in 1961, Allen and Connie discovered the federal government was offering the opportunity to acquire 160 acres of land in Alaska by homesteading. They decided to apply and were granted the opportunity to homestead in Goldstream Valley some five miles from University of Alaska in Fairbanks. In order to fulfill the requirements for a land patent that assigns ownership of a tract of land there, they were required to live on the land a minimum of seven months a year for three years, plant and raise a grain crop on a minimum of 10 acres and build a habitable house.

Their decision to file for a homestead seemed almost inevitable considering that Connie's grandfather had homesteaded in Iowa when he immigrated from Norway and her own father came from that homestead in Iowa to claim his own homestead in Montana. This makes Connie the third generation to homestead in her family. The pioneering spirit runs deep in her genetic makeup.

Clearing, Cabin, and Crop

During the fall of 1962 they began the hard work of clearing their claim. With the muscle of a bulldozer, the trees and tundra brush were pushed into big piles like a farm windrow, a two-month long project, working every day. Just as the first snow fell, the huge pile was set on fire and burned for a long time, almost the entire winter.

Even though the Homesteading Act didn't require that the crop had to grow, the next spring they planted Norwegian oats by hand on this cleared land, a tried and tested crop in a similar environment that they knew would grow in Alaska. The federal government's Bureau of Land Management came and inspected to make sure a crop had been planted.

With no requirement to market their crop, the oats became food for the moose and birds.

The other requirement was to build a habitable house. Winter was coming, so the cabin was built rather quickly. They started the three-month task of building a 16' x 24' two-story, two-room log cabin with the help of a friend who owned a lumber company. The second story was reached with a ladder through a hole in the ceiling. They had electricity but water had to be brought in from Fairbanks using Ace Hardware five-gallon buckets. Living in a cabin they built themselves with an outhouse and no running water, and heating the cabin with wood, was all very similar to how Connie grew up, so she didn't think too much about it—that's just the way it was. This cozy cabin was ready to move into by the fall of 1962.

When they had successfully completed all the requirements for the patent, the homestead was theirs. Their patent was signed and recorded by the Bureau of Land Management in Anchorage on January 4, 1967, showing that they were the first owners of this homestead claim.

Homestead Living

Some small openings in the outer cabin walls did not seem significant at the time of the hasty construction, but when the inevitable cold weather arrived, the small openings became an issue. One morning they woke up to a squirrel at the foot of their bed looking them in the eye. The openings were quickly filled in to prevent these visitors from rudely barging in again. Even so, Connie complained when her mixer beaters and some pieces of her silverware were missing. Sometime later Al climbed a fir tree to remove branches when he spied the silverware and mixer beaters in the squirrel nest. Mystery solved! Connie was never very fond of squirrels from that day on!!

The first winter was exceptionally cold with temperatures plummeting to 50 and 60 degrees below zero. To stay warm, the cabin was heated with wood, and they made sure the big wood stove was well stocked. Little did they know the effect the heat would have on the entire cabin though. In the spring it became evident that the house had literally tilted during the winter as the heat from this wood stove thawed the permafrost below, causing the cabin to settle, sinking into the permafrost. With ice on his shoes, the linoleum floor became a bit like a skating rink as Al slid from one end of the cabin to the other on the smooth now-slanted floor.

Because this area had never been settled before, there was only one primitive road to the cabin. Using a Ford Bronco, they traveled over a soupy bog daily as they traveled back and forth to their teaching jobs in Fairbanks. In fact, it took three vehicles to get to school—the four-wheel drive Bronco through the bog, a Scout from the edge of the bog to town, then catching a ride with other teachers to their respective schools. The Goldstream bog was so soupy that, to keep from sinking into it, they often quickly raced the Bronco over the ground. The flying mud decorated their clothing in socially unacceptable ways so that they kept clean clothes at school in order to be presentable to their classes.

They were not alone in this transportation adventure as two other families also homesteaded in this area. As is necessary in this type of environment, they helped each other in many ways including traversing this bog. Besides the bog hindering transportation, the extreme temperatures made it difficult for vehicles to get started, another reason they sometimes provided transportation for the other homesteaders.

During the extremely cold days of winter, homesteaders employed a variety of ways to get their vehicles started. Because some of them had no electricity to keep vehicle components warm, they used some rather risky tricks to try to get them going. Al, like many others, put gasoline in a coffee can, threw a match into it, and slid the burning gasoline under the oil pan of the vehicle to warm the oil. This would only work if it was -50 degrees or colder because gas fumes cannot vaporize and rise at that temperature. One neighbor tried to warm the oil in his vehicle with a weed burner, running it under the oil pan. He soon found out what a bad idea this was when the vehicle caught fire and was totally destroyed. There was no way the fire department could come to this very remote part of Alaska. Sometimes Al and Connie put their car battery in their warm oven so that it had the power to turn the motor over—a far safer method.

Besides the bog and the difficulty of getting vehicles started, the onset of the long winter in October brought a whole set of other problems. Just keeping the log cabin warm enough to live in required constant care and attention. To save money, they used wood that they cut themselves to heat their cabin. Unfortunately, during the day while they were gone and not able to feed the wood stove, the inside of the cabin cooled down, often to 18 degrees, well below freezing. This presented another problem–keeping food from freezing! In order to prevent that, they kept food in their large refrigerator at 40 degrees.

When their first wedding anniversary rolled around in June 1962, they were stuck at the homestead with no place to go. Literally stuck. Not even a four-wheel drive vehicle would get through the rain-saturated muskeg and bog that surrounded them. They were disappointed that they were not able to do anything to get away for a while. But such is life in extreme remote areas.

The Thompson Fairbanks homestead cabin after 60 years. Photo credit Mike Flodin.

"Outside" Friends

When one is in Alaska, anyone who is not from Alaska is considered to be from "outside." If one leaves Alaska for any reason, then one is going "outside." One of the couples from "outside" that Allen and Connie got to know well and who quickly became best friends were Sheila and Dennis Weston. They were both first-year teachers when they arrived in Fairbanks as newlyweds in August 1963. When they arrived in Fairbanks, the Thompsons took them under their wing with their welcoming ways. Sheila particularly needed this as she had grown up in the city and had never been so far from home and needed this friendship and support.

Sheila, the city girl, says in her own words that she was mortified when she saw her new home in this old rundown dusty town. She sat down and cried and would have willingly turned around and gone back home if that had been possible. Their friendship with the Thompsons helped ease the pain of this move. They rented a basement apartment close to downtown, which was adequate, but not great. But when she compared her new home to the Thompsons, Sheila saw her place in a new light. The Thompsons were in a two-story two-room cabin on a desolate road outside of Fairbanks with no indoor plumbing, only a wood-fire stove for heat, and living a very primitive lifestyle.

Another horrifying aspect of Alaska that Sheila as well as many other unseasoned cheechakos (Alaskan term for a tenderfoot newcomer) who came to the Last Frontier were not prepared for was the slaughter and butchering of animals. She was not from a hunting family and had never seen an animal butchered. She had never even given it much thought, but if she had, she says she would have figured that the animals whose meat shows up in those packages in the grocery store just volunteered to be there.

Sheila was horrified after a hunt when the dead moose was dragged through another teacher's house who had agreed that, for a share of the meat, he would let them cut up the meat at his house. Dennis, Wesley and Al drug the smelly carcass through the living room all the way to a back area of the house where sawhorses and plywood were set up, ready for the butchering. The three of them hacked away at the poor moose with saws and knives, unaffected by the gross scene. Sheila was dumbfounded and sad for the moose, but it didn't seem to affect Connie who had grown up on the farm.

When Sheila discovered the women were expected to help package the moose, her nausea would not allow her to even get close. Allen was so kind and sensitive to her feelings that he assured her she was not required to help. Sheila will never forget how kind and wonderful Al was during this traumatic event. This is another reason why Connie and Al became irreplaceable friends.

Hunting Near Disaster and Birthday Disappointment

Al enjoyed hunting and did so every weekend for 20 weeks in a row. The quality of this wild game meat was questionable until research showed that the Chinese bomb and subsequent radioactive material in the cloud that drifted across the Bering Sea and over Alaska in the 1960s affected the caribou horns, but not the meat. Al hunted way more meat than they could possibly use, so they gave the excess away to the other teachers. He shot moose and caribou, and trapped foxes and wolverines. They had the hides tanned and sold them for extra money.

One particular hunting trip on a September weekend in 1963 nearly ended in disaster. Al enjoyed hunting, but his new friend, Dennis, *loved* hunting! Al, always the educator, took Dennis and another teacher friend, Don, north on the Steese Highway, a scenic and historic road that goes to within 50 miles of the Arctic Circle. There were several springs near the roadbed and, if they were large enough, the water would cross the road forming an ice slick that must be driven over. The safest way to traverse these icy patches was with a good set of studded tires.

Fortunately, the men had dressed for the weather. Their arctic gear consisted of insulated pants, mukluks, gloves with a second pair of arctic gloves on top of them, fur lined Air Force all-weather arctic jackets with hoods that had a ruff of wolverine fur that rolled out six to eight inches from their faces. (Wolverine fur is preferred by residents of the Far North for hood ruffs as it makes it easy to brush off the accumulated frost before it melts, helping to keep the wearer dry and more comfortable.) They would soon find out how essential all this gear was for their survival.

Hunting for the moose was the easiest part of this trip. At fifty below zero, Al remembers seeing the shockwave of the bullet traveling toward the moose, the only time he ever witnessed this phenomenon. After successfully shooting the moose, they field dressed their kill before loading it into Al's Scout. The cold caused the moose's blood to freeze onto the men's hands almost instantly so that they found it necessary to keep their hands inside the moose's body cavity as much as possible to be able to keep working.

With the meat loaded into Al's Scout, the men started the drive back to Fairbanks. They were about 40 miles out of Fairbanks when the wheels spun out on an ice pack formed by one of those springs. The Scout went into the ditch backwards with the nose of the vehicle pointed up, a disaster for anyone anywhere. However, at 50 below zero and 40 miles from town on a sparsely traveled road, the men knew they were in serious trouble. Their only option was to start walking toward town although they knew their chances of survival were very small if they would have to walk the whole distance. Having driven down the highway a number of times, they were familiar with the territory and knew there were cabins along the way that could possibly provide some temporary refuge.

They were thankful when, about five miles down the road, nearly exhausted and feeling the effects of the cold, they finally came upon a log cabin. However, it was so old and broken down that they couldn't stay in it without freezing even though it did still have some beds inside. With severely limited options, this was where they needed to stay for the night. The roof had caved in and the walls were sagging badly on one side. It was in such a state of disrepair that they knew no one would ever attempt to repair this derelict old cabin, so they turned it into firewood. In order to survive the frigid night, they set fire to the whole cabin.

In order to lie down with as much comfort and safety as possible, they stomped on the snow around the edge of the fire perimeter. They laid down in the snow to sleep, their warm arctic clothing doing its job of keeping their body heat close to their bodies. Even though they were lying down right on the snow, their coats did not get wet from their body heat melting the snow. One can only imagine how uncomfortable and unsettling sleeping under these conditions had to be.

Meanwhile, back in Fairbanks the three wives were waiting for Allen, Dennis and Don to return. Connie and Sheila both had birthdays that week and had worked to scrape together the money to purchase four tickets to eat at the nicest restaurant in town, the Switzerland. The tickets were prepaid and non-refundable and in Al's pocket far from Fairbanks, of no use to anyone. The men had promised to be back, but the women had no way of knowing what had happened to them to keep them away from this important pre-arranged date. The women waited and waited at the Weston apartment. Sheila was getting angrier by the minute although Connie seemed to be calm.

The next morning, Connie, who actually was frantic with worry, sent some friends up the road to look for the men. Early in the morning and several hours before sunup on this long Arctic night, the men were elated to see their rescuers coming down the road. The rescuers found the stranded hunters near the cabin that had now been reduced to a stack of dying embers. Their rescuers were thankful to find the missing men in good condition and quickly loaded them up to drive them back to the safety of a warm home and the welcome embrace of their frantic wives.

Later the men returned to the vehicle and pulled it out of the ditch using a homestead jack with a cable clamped onto the hook and another onto the lifting nose as a winch. The three men, working together, were able to lift the Scout back up onto the road, a task that took all day. Once back to civilization, they took the truck to a repair garage where they parked it, with the moose still firmly frozen and immovable inside. It took about a week for the moose to thaw out enough to be removed, blood dripping out of the carcass and into the seats (that later had to be replaced) and onto the plastic tarp stretched beneath the vehicle.

That was a really close call! If it weren't for that cabin, they would never have made it. Even this episode did not deter the men from hunting weekend after weekend. But they never ever took their wives to eat at the Switzerland!

Earthquake!

Another day that will be etched into Al and Connie's memories for as long as they live is Good Friday, March 27, 1964. On that day, the most powerful earthquake in U.S. history, and the second largest ever recorded, shook Alaska for over four and a half minutes at 5:36 p.m. The 9.2 magnitude earthquake was centered in Prince William Sound, closer to Anchorage than Fairbanks but the tremor was felt there while Al was driving to pick up Connie at the laundromat. The pavement was shaking and rolling in waves so that Al had to get out of the vehicle. They ran to each other and held tight, convinced it was the end of the world! All communication with the lower 48 was disrupted for days.

At the time, Al was with the Anchorage Air National Guard. They were called to active duty to guard heavily damaged downtown Anchorage from any trespassers. It took about a week before the police took over security in the area. Al's memories of the unbelievable damage in Anchorage include a tall spruce tree growing right on the line where the earth split. The tree, in the cold, had split from top to bottom, part sliding one direction and the other half sliding in the opposite direction. It was quite the sight! The Catholic hospital pancaked right to the ground, but the elevator shaft stood tall in the midst of the wreckage. When Al flew back to Fairbanks, he looked down on the Turnagain Arm residential neighborhood that had slid into the ocean and saw the chimneys of the houses sticking up out of the water, an eerie and horrible sight.

The effects of this devastating earthquake were still visible decades after it happened. As recently as 2015, Al and his friends Dennis and Don were invited onto a friend's boat who took them from Whittier into Prince William Sound. He wanted them to see a bit of evidence of the power of the tsunami that occurred after the earthquake. They went to a place where a big V was visible in the tree line from the island shore and half way up its hillside. When they got off the boat and explored the area, they found a section of a huge dock, part of a pier that had broken loose when the tsunami ripped it out from its moorings and carried it 40 miles or more, hurling it up onto the island with enough force that it crashed through the trees and tore them up, creating this V-shaped clearing. In the intervening years, trees had started to grow through the pier, now setting on land. The men were impressed by this evidence of the strength of an earthquake that could cause such a powerful tsunami.

The End of Homesteading

During their last year in Fairbanks, they purchased what they affectionately refer to as the "Aluminum Tube," a 40-foot by 8-foot Airstream trailer for $2400. Connie even had her piano in it which helped pass the time while they lived in it. Al and Connie left the Fairbanks homestead shortly after the earthquake, moving to Anchorage in July 1964 partly because they were both tired of the cold which is much more intense in the Fairbanks area. In addition, they agreed that homesteading in this climate was more work than they anticipated.

They subdivided their claim several years later when they realized it was a prime time for development of Fairbanks during the pipeline-building era that would not last forever. They named all the streets except for one that they forgot about–they told an engineer to name the street and he gave it the questionable name "Yellowsnow Road"--and to their amazement, the City of Fairbanks okayed that name. As it turns out, this is a favorite place for tourists to get their photos taken!

Life in Anchorage after the earthquake took quite a few months to return to normal. They lived in the Aluminum Tube for two years after they moved there, an inexpensive way to live in this city that was still suffering the ravages of destruction. When Al and Connie got there in the fall, many of the schools had suffered damage from the earthquake and had to "double shift," with some classes being held from 7:00 a.m. to noon and some from 12:15 p.m. to 5:00 p.m. This gave Al and Connie time to work on and earn their Master's degrees from University of Alaska.

CHAPTER 5

MORE PIECES OF ALASKA

Loon Lake

Of course, outgoing and friendly Connie and Allen met new friends when they moved to Anchorage in the fall of 1964. Among them were Connie Maxey and her husband, Joe, who also came to Anchorage in the fall of that year. They were all teachers, and the two Connie's taught in the same school. They and a few other teachers became good friends and did many things together. The husbands had similar interests and the men spent many weekends in the great Alaskan outdoors. This friendship later provided an opportunity for a couple of joint ventures.

As if the homestead that they worked diligently to claim had not been enough of a challenge, the Thompsons, along with Connie and Joe, pursued yet another opportunity. The State of Alaska was giving away parcels of land that, unlike the work required for a homestead, only required an official survey and some paperwork to claim. Of course, they could not let this opportunity to leave more footprints pass them by!

Joe and Al purchased snow machines (called snowmobiles most places other than Alaska), an exciting way to go out and explore, and that they did just about every weekend. Al and Joe found Loon Lake, a small lake off the road system near Talkeetna, surrounded by some of this free land, and accessible by float plane. Several other people had the same idea and had already staked claims at the other end of the lake.

Allen, Joe and a couple of their other teacher friends staked out their 5-acre plots pretty much all on the same weekend in 1969. The land could not be permanently claimed until it was surveyed, but no one had the money to hire a surveyor to fly to this remote area. This was not a big problem as the State would allow one to continue to keep one's claim until able to get it surveyed—for an annual fee, of course.

Finally, by 1974 there were enough people who had staked out their plots so that they were able to pool their resources, fly a surveyor in to survey all the plots at one time, pay the $400 patent fee to the State of Alaska, and these recreation sites were theirs with no other requirements to fulfill. There still is no road, but a float plane can land on Loon Lake, or one can hike or take a snow machine on one of the meandering trails that go around a lake and through a swamp, probably four to five miles. Al and Connie did not often go to this claim but they did enjoy an occasional snow machine ride there and hunted in the area.

The era of free land eventually had to come to an end. The last Alaska homestead was patented in 1988. In fact, that was the last homestead in the whole United States.

Painter Creek Lodge

One of Joe's friends, JW, became one of the founders of Painter Creek Lodge (in the middle of the Alaska Peninsula) when the property was purchased for $100,000 by four partners in June 1982. JW was a lot like Allen—he was talkative and knew many people. When the property went up for sale, JW thought it would be a great spot for a fishing lodge.

The lodge is on 15 acres of land overlooking the King Salmon River and Painter Creek, south of the village of King Salmon near Aniakchak volcano. This ideally positioned property is adjacent to a 4000-foot runway, built in the 1950s when oil companies were busy exploring for oil in that area. Joe was a vocational education teacher at the King Center in the Anchorage School District teaching building construction. This construction experience was ideal for the renovations and additions needed on the property that already had a small cabin near the runway, another building that could later be used for the supplies needed for working on airplanes or improvements to the property, a main lodge building that required some additions and renovations, and a couple of cabins down the trail from the runway that could be used for guests.

When looking for partners, JW chose Joe because of his building experience, another partner flew planes and could be used to fly clients in and out, and an attorney was chosen to be the fourth partner because of his ability to make sure things were all done legally. JW was the manager and marketer who went out and found customers.

The Lodge struggled for the first few years until things were built and in place. They averaged only 6-10 clients the first few summers. Running the Lodge was exhausting with little financial reward so that, one by one, the original partners left until Joe was left to be the manager. Shortly after this, Allen visited and became interested in being involved with the Lodge. He bought some shares along with a couple of other people and became an important voice in the annual shareholders' meetings as a member of the board, helping manage this enterprise, and finding clients by going to sportsmen's shows in the lower 48.

Shortly after Allen became part owner with Joe, the State of Alaska, the Alaska Natives and the federal government divided the State of Alaska into thirds. The Native corporations, the State and the federal government each got one third of the land. Coincidentally Jimmy Carter, the President at the time of this division, liked to fish in the area. Because of this interest, he established Aniakchak National Monument adjacent to Painter Creek Lodge, about 450 miles south of Anchorage. The Monument includes two volcanoes, one of which is still active today and that Al and Connie explored. This ideal location, privately owned land near the National Monument, the two rivers emptying into Bristol Bay and surrounded by peaks of the Aleutian Range, helped the Painter Creek Lodge to become the dominant fishing lodge in the Aniakchak region, truly one of a kind.

Some of the many repeat clients at Painter Creek Lodge were the Johnny Cash family who went there for three years. Johnny himself did not like to fish, but he wanted his wife, June Carter Cash, and their son, John, to learn how to fish. John wasn't interested in fishing as much as June so he spent his time driving clients back and forth to the river.

Besides trying to build a dependable clientele and making a profit, running a fishing lodge in a remote area had other challenges. A caretaker could not always be hired to keep an eye on things in the off-season. During one off-season incident, a bear got into the kitchen, knocked out windows, scratched doors, smashed the freezer, and caused quite a bit of other damage. A volcanic eruption closed the Lodge down for at least two seasons because the ash disrupted the fish migration. The covid pandemic also affected the numbers of clients.

Tragedy struck in 2000 when Joe, a skilled pilot, flying home from a fishing expedition, flew into a cloud bank and crashed into a mountain. Joe and two other fishermen were killed in the crash. After this disaster, Allen was a great support to Joe's wife, Connie, who is still a shareholder. The first season after this disaster, he also helped serve as a guide for customers who had already booked for that season. Eventually, Al sold his interest in the Lodge to Joe's wife. In spite of these difficulties, the Lodge still serves fishermen every year where they catch king, red and silver salmon, rainbow trout and grayling, without having to seek out other locations that provide this variety of fish.

CHAPTER 6

FINDING THE REAL ALLEN THOMPSON

The Thompsons lived a financially conservative life for several years, teaching school and saving up in order to be able to afford to buy a house. Finally, in 1967, they were able to move out of the Aluminum Tube (which they sold for $2400, the same amount they had paid for it several years before) and purchase a real house, a beautiful 2500-square-foot home for the amazing price of $30,000, the going price for a home in the Sand Lake Area of Anchorage, near where Connie was teaching at the time. Her youngest sister, Mary Marie, also a teacher, and her two-year-old daughter lived with Al and Connie while her husband was in the Army, stationed in Vietnam. Their second year in this home, her sister Norma came to live with them for a year while she was teaching in Anchorage. This home had a well-used welcome mat.

In 1969 Al and Connie planned a dream vacation to Australia's Great Barrier Reef, Fiji, and Tahiti to go scuba diving at these favorite places of divers, a perfect challenge for these two diving enthusiasts. As a way to finance this vacation, they advertised to rent their lovely warm and hospitable Anchorage house that they loved so much while they were gone. In preparation for this glorious trip, Al and Connie moved their personal belongings including bank records, their 12-piece set of sterling silver from Connie's mother that they received as a wedding gift as well as most of their other wedding gifts, and all of Allen's guns into the garage and locked it securely, sure it would all be safe and sound while they were at the other end of the earth. Allen's trophy mounted and stuffed sheep head was securely hanging on their living room wall. They had even hired their 12-year-old neighborhood twins to come over to mow the lawn each week. With every detail in place, they thought they were ready to enjoy a carefree trip, never once expecting this to be the beginning of a terrifying roller coaster ride.

They then left for Australia and the magnificent diving opportunities that Australia presented, with renters, who had paid one month's rent and a deposit in cash, happily living in their home. Two months passed while Al and Connie were enjoying many undersea marvels. They watched the moon landing while in Sidney, Australia. Eventually the Thompsons needed more money but when they called their bank, they found out that there was no money in their bank account! Already having a return ticket, they quickly returned to Alaska intending to find out why they had no money.

The first thing they did was call the police who informed them that they had been looking for Allen. Supposedly he had rented a big trailer a few days before and had never returned it. After several minutes of explaining that he had certainly not rented a trailer that had not been returned, the officer took them to the FBI to talk to them about the increasingly alarming situation. When they left the FBI office, they had a ticket on their windshield even though the car had been parked perfectly in a legal parking zone. The problem was that there was no license plate! It, too, had been stolen.

Identity theft was not common in these times, and many safeguards now in place were unheard of then. With few safeguards in place, their renter and his pregnant wife turned out to be successful liars, swindlers, and thieves who managed to make Al and Connie's lives miserable for the next few years.

Back at their house, they discovered the further horrific news that it had been completely cleared out—no furniture or personal belongings remained. They discovered that everything that had been securely locked in the garage was gone including their school diplomas, marriage license, and check books. The thieves had gone through all their mail and cashed every check that had come in their absence. Allen's National Guard checks had been cashed, and his federal firearms certificate was gone. When they checked their burn barrel behind the house, there were pages of what were obviously practice signatures, the thieves trying to identically copy their legal signatures. On their way out of town, the thieves had stopped at the Thompsons' bank in Palmer and withdrew all their money, except for twenty cents.

The swindler, whom we shall call "X", was able to go to the Department of Motor Vehicles and easily obtain an Alaska driver's license with Allen's name on it. At this time, Alaska licenses did not have a photo of the person on them, making it fairly easy to pull off this deception. X then went to the post office and changed the delivery of Al and Connie's mail to come back to their Anchorage house where X could easily take care of whatever illegal business he intended to, unhindered. Having assumed Al's identity, he began a methodical plan to sell everything he could. Bank of America gave him a high balance credit card which he used with great abandon, knowing he would not ever pay the bill. After staying in the Thompson's house for two months, X and his wife left Anchorage for the lower 48, hoping to disappear.

X traveled all over the central United States using the Bank of America credit card with Allen Thompson's unsullied reputation linked to it. Because there was no system set up to shut off the use of credit cards in those days, X was able to buy cars and stay in fancy hotels with no hindrance. Eventually X had charged over $100,000 before the police were able to catch him.

The detective assigned to their case had Al and Connie pick up their mail daily as X was using the Bank of America and Chevron gas credit cards to travel with. They were able to trace his travels on a map of the United States using receipts to find where he last stopped. They would often get irate phone calls from casinos, restaurants and hotels wondering when outstanding bills would be paid. The detective took these calls and told them the charges were part of a fraudulent operation.

Meanwhile one of the bills they received from his escapades was from an Alaska hospital for the birth of the X baby whom they named Connie. Years later Al and Connie received a call from the Royal Canadian Mounted Police. They had found Al and Connie's marriage license and college diplomas inside a wrecked trailer near White Horse, Yukon, Canada.

X was finally apprehended after six months on the run. He had 22 license plates in his possession, stolen off of rental cars from across the nation. When apprehended in another state, X asserted he was the real Allen Thompson, so the next day the FBI showed up at Al's place of employment at West Anchorage High School. They finger printed Allen to see who the real Allen Thompson was. Once the real Allen Thompson was identified, the imposter was quickly extradited to Anchorage where he was incarcerated. If only this was the end of the story, but X was not one to give up easily.

X was assigned a public defender who put up bail money. X, unhindered by any kind of conscience, fled the state of Alaska. This slippery character was caught in Canada, tried, convicted, and sentenced within 30 days of his arrest as required by Canadian law, and spent three years in a Canadian prison.

When X was released in Canada after serving this three-year sentence, the State of Alaska met him and extradited him back to Alaska where he was convicted of fraud and sentenced to 12 more years in prison. And that concluded his crime spree at the Thompsons' expense although it took years to recover from this financial fiasco.

CHAPTER 7

BUILDING A FAMILY

Bill and A Little Girl–1973–The Rescue

In 1973 Al and Connie had been married 12 years and were teaching in Anchorage but were given a sabbatical leave for a year to study at University of Southern California at Los Angeles. That year changed their family for the rest of their lives, the highlight of their lives up to this point.

There is no such thing as coincidence, only God's timing. When they were watching a television program about adoption, two children's faces appeared on the screen. Connie suggested they contact the agency to consider adopting these two children. A quick phone call brought them into the social worker's office.

Although they initially asked for younger children, the social workers realized that with their experiences and teaching older children, they had the ability to parent older kids. The faces they saw belonged to a 13-year-old boy and an 8-year-old girl who had spent many years, always together, in foster homes. Wards of the state, there were no opportunities for them to be placed together in foster care. Since Al and Connie were willing to take both of the children and were from out of state, the social workers expedited the adoption process. It took a whole week of physically carrying paperwork from office to office to expedite this process and within three months, Bill and the little girl were officially part of the Thompson family.

After finishing the year working on their university studies and spending all their free time getting to know Bill and their daughter, assuring them that they finally had a permanent home, it was time to return to Alaska. They left their apartment that was only a few blocks from the ocean in Santa Monica, and drove 4,500 miles in their 24-foot Winnebago from Los Angeles to Anchorage with both children who had never been out of the greater Los Angeles city limits. A stop in Montana to meet their new extended family, Al's family in western Montana and Connie's family in eastern Montana, was quite an experience for these two who had been raised in the inner city. Bill was stunned by all the wide-open spaces and had his first driving lesson with his grandfather in a pickup truck with a stick shift. Their daughter was introduced to horses which later became an important part of her life.

When the family got to Anchorage, Bill and their daughter were enrolled in school and lived in their Winnebago for several months until they acquired their home on West 23rd Avenue in Anchorage. Al and Connie went back to teaching for one more year, then resigned to go into business full time, managing an 18-unit apartment building, and the task of learning how to be parents to two children who had never had parents, an exhausting experience for all of them. When Bill had an expensive down winter jacket stolen, Connie said, "Oh, Bill. That is probably the nicest thing you have ever had!" But Bill immediately replied, "No! You guys are!" What a reward for all the love invested into these two "throw away" kids.

Bill did well in school and loved sports and eventually became an outstanding basketball player for West Anchorage High School. He initially entered the business world, managing bowling companies in Anchorage, Waco, Chicago, St. Louis, and the Philippines. After doing that for ten years, he returned to Alaska and became an honor student at Alaska Pacific University. Today Bill is a special needs teacher in Los Angeles. Bill and his wife Magumi had two children.

Their daughter attended a private school through eighth grade, then attended Service High School until the family moved to the North Slope. She found school on the North Slope to be too dramatic a change from what she was used to. After about a half year, she finished her last three years of high school in Livermore, California, with Connie's sister. She took horseback riding lessons and owned her own horse when she was 16 years old. She became the state champion equestrian rider when she was a high school senior as well as a state champion western pleasure horseback rider, winning many ribbons at the Alaska State Fair.

A few years ago, Bill told his mom and dad that when they crossed the border between Montana and Canada, he knew this adoption would stick as it was too far to take them back again. What a joyful feeling that had to be for these young children who lacked security for so many years. Statistically, children in their situation either end up homeless, in jail, or dead within three years.

Michael–1979

April 1979 brought another burst of joy into their lives, just when they were in desperate need of it. Michael came into their family during an extremely stressful time, probably the lowest summer of their lives. Yet, it was also the best time as they needed something joyous to help them bear the burdens and stress of their situation. Their businesses were struggling, and the storms of life were getting stronger and scarier. This was the year the Thompsons had been forced into bankruptcy. For the second time, everything had been taken from them except each other and their children.

The idea was planted to adopt another child a few years earlier while Al was working as a special needs teacher in a program for disadvantaged kids. Al's associate, Joann, knew that they wanted to adopt again, and encouraged them to work with Catholic Charities in Anchorage. At this point in their lives, they were in their mid-40s and considered too old to be adopting an infant. It was a sad day when Catholic Charities said "No" to their adoption inquiry. Joann, however, was a strong Catholic and would not take NO for an answer. She called the archbishop personally and pleaded their case.

One week later, Al and Connie were in a counseling program for adoptive parents. A few months after that, they were introduced to their social worker, a delightful person who understood all their needs. Michael came to them when he was 19 days old. The night they went to Catholic Social Services to pick up Michael and take him home as their own, they came out to find their car was gone–repossessed!

Within a few months, the Thompson family was on their way to Anaktuvuk Pass, to good paying jobs that would be a step toward financial recovery. With the help of God, supportive friends, a strong work ethic and commitment to each other, they were able to eventually work their way out of this challenging set of circumstances.

Allen and Connie were convinced there is no such thing as coincidence, and they agreed that the gift of Michael that tumultuous summer was perfect timing. He brought them so much joy and helped to take their minds off their financial troubles. These circumstances also put them right back into the classroom, the place where they belonged and where they could use their God-given talents.

Michael went on to become an award-winning competitive swimmer during his preteen and early teen years when he, Allen and Connie lived in Indonesia. He kept swimming when he was a high school student and they all lived in Homer, Alaska. After graduation and trying his hand at various jobs, he became a massage therapist. He married and had one daughter.

CHAPTER 8

THE LANDLORDS

In 1974, the Thompsons were living in Anchorage and had been making good money with their teaching jobs, enjoying being new parents to Bill and their daughter. Life was going well but then Allen, always looking for a new challenge, thought investing into properties was a good idea. He had been inspired by the book by Bill Nickerson, *How I Turned $1,000 into a Million*. After a visit with the author while they were in California, in 1975 they quit their teaching jobs and purchased an 18-apartment building in downtown Anchorage.

This old building, Dolando Apartments, was constructed in the mid-1930s, and was one of the most unique buildings in downtown Anchorage, complete with an interesting history. It had been used during World War II as a military transit point by pilots who traveled between Russia and the United States. Al discovered this while remodeling when he found hammer and sickle insignias of the Communist party burned into the support posts along with names of Russian pilots. Further research revealed that pilots lived in this building during the war exchange program when Russian pilots would fly airplanes from Anchorage to Russia.

During the next four to five years, they continued to invest in properties until eventually they acquired 81 apartments, a trailer park, and a water utility, all in Anchorage. After tying up so much of their assets into the real estate market, there was a serious downturn in the post-pipeline era. This, combined with their lack of experience in this financial world that led them to overextend themselves, brought them to a place where they could no longer continue to run these businesses and were forced to declare bankruptcy. This was to be a long and humiliating period in their lives.

Connie always knew that Al was a strong and good person, traits that attracted him to her in the first place. However, in the face of this financial crisis, with seemingly endless lawsuits and bad checks, she could not avoid listening to the many people who were encouraging her to consider divorce. That possibility had occurred to her and she had seriously considered it, but when looking into the future, she could not imagine going on without Allen by her side. It was during this struggle that Connie's good friend Shirley flew to Anchorage to counsel and pray with them in a beautiful soft snow storm outside a downtown restaurant. Shirley knew both Al and Connie well and did not want to see their marriage destroyed. She reminded them that bankruptcy could take everything away from them, but not what was in their heads. This was the encouragement they needed to hear to point them back to doing what they both knew to do best–teaching! With this timely reminder, Connie and Al decided to go back into teaching, taking jobs on the North Slope.

Because they once again had good salaries with these teaching jobs, they were able to find a knowledgeable lawyer who was willing to take their case even though their reputations were suffering greatly because of the debt. They acknowledge that God had a plan for them, stopping them from getting into even worse trouble, redirecting them back into their chosen careers, and investing themselves into parenthood.

Although the financial repercussions of this bankruptcy would pursue them even to the North Slope for several years, with the help of their lawyer, they were eventually able to work their way out of the tangle of debt. All debts were repaid within a few years and they were living a much happier life, thriving in their profession. This deeply humiliating disaster in the summer of 1979 changed their lives and directed their footprints in a wonderful direction.

CHAPTER 9

WILDERNESS RAFTING

The Raft

Avon rafts have been made famous because of their role in many accounts of survival at sea. An Avon raft was instrumental in saving the lives of one man who was adrift on the Atlantic Ocean for 76 days. Two sailors survived in their Avon raft for 13 days after abandoning ship in a 1981 incident. (https://en.wikipedia.org/wiki/Avon Inflatables) The Avon company itself claims that their rafts have been involved with more successful rescues than any other, including a rescue after 117 days (http://www. avoninflatables.co.uk/page/oac).

Al often seemed to be in the right place at the right time, and the opportunity to become the owner of an Avon raft was one of those times. In the early 1960s, he was able to purchase a 10-man Avon raft when the company was just getting started and was shipping one raft to each state.

Al just happened to be at Alaska Marine in Anchorage when they got theirs, and he immediately snatched it up. This raft became the vehicle for many float trips down the Kenai River, the Kobuk River in the Arctic, the Fortymile and Yukon Rivers in eastern Alaska, as well as rivers in the lower 48.

When the family is reminiscing about raft trips, two of them immediately come to mind–one, a trip that could have ended tragically, and the other a trip of a lifetime for a young man and his family.

It Could Have Been a Lot Worse

This story is not about a rescue at sea, but it **is** a story that required a rescue, and it **is** about an incident with an Avon raft.

Allen and Connie had floated down a great easy-flowing river on the Kenai Peninsula in their raft before. Their glowing reports about this fun and easy trip convinced five of their friends and their niece, Kathy, who was visiting from Montana, to join them in their raft on a warm Sunday morning in 1971. However, they had not taken into consideration the fact that there had been significant rains that week. In addition to the rain, the warm temperatures added a large amount of glacial melt water to the creeks and rivers in the area.

The North Fork River in Turnagain Pass on the Kenai Peninsula was their destination. The river normally flows at 13 miles per hour, a fast current by rafting standards. This current and the bloated river did not give them any time to react to the sight of two very large trees blocking the surface of the entire width of the river, visible only after they came around a curve in the river. The only thing they could do was crash into the downed trees which abruptly stopped the raft while the current tipped the raft backwards, dumping all its occupants into the deep water, fighting the rapid current.

Immediately all eight passengers were pulled underwater and dragged beneath the trees with their tangled roots dangling into the water. Connie and Kathy were able to grab hold onto a branch and hold on. Connie remembers that she could not have held on much longer as the strong current was trying to pull her away. Al, the hero of this story and a strong swimmer, was able to swim over to where Connie and Kathy, the only women on this expedition, were hanging on with all their strength. He picked up Connie and took her to the safety of shore, then returned to rescue Kathy. The other five passengers made their way to shore, wet and cold, shaken and frightened, with billfolds and other personal possessions long gone, claimed by the water as its toll for releasing them from its clutches.

Miraculously, all of them were able to return to the raft and finish the float trip. If they had known about the trees blocking the river, they never would have started this particular adventure. This is yet another example of how God was certainly with them, watching over them in a dangerous situation. This incident was a great topic of conversation for a long time afterwards.

Fortymile River Exploration

It was in 1975, just a couple of years after Bill and the little girl were adopted by Al and Connie and taken out of California, that the family went on a raft trip that Bill, 15 years old at the time, will never forget.

The Thompson family lived in their 24-foot Winnebago motorhome when they moved back to Alaska. This was the perfect home to get them to some interesting and fairly remote areas. Along with some friends, Ben and Peggy and their family, they planned a memorable raft trip. They drove to an historic area where Alaska's first major gold rush occurred in 1886 and put their big rubber rafts into the Fortymile River, an eastern Alaska tributary of the Yukon River. The river was named by the gold prospectors during those gold rush days.

As they floated down the river, they saw remnants of the history of this area in the old cabins the fur trappers and gold prospectors left behind as well as relics of mining days abandoned along its banks. They decided to investigate one cabin, and when they entered it, they noted that layers of newspapers were nailed to the ceiling, perhaps for insulation against the brutal winters in this Alaskan interior area. Closer inspection revealed that these newspapers dated back to the 1800s and hadn't been touched for years. A very old 1924 calendar hung on the wall, opened to the month of December, with all the dates crossed off right up to December 24. This led to some speculation about what happened to the cabin's inhabitants after that.

Back behind the cabin, Bill spied some rusty metal sticking out of the ground. They dug it up and found it to be an old rusty rifle barrel. An exploration of the woods surrounding the cabin yielded a huge antique wagon wheel, complete with its metal rim and the spokes in good condition, no rust or rot. Of course, they had to take these artifacts back to Anchorage—Al wanted to use them to decorate their house— so they loaded them onto the back of the raft. They were quite the sight floating down the river with a huge wagon wheel hanging off the back of the raft.

The families had packed tents and supplies for camping. Their first night out was very cold, even though it was summer. They were happy to see another deserted cabin, a welcome alternative to camping in the cold. It was so cold that Bill was crying. His socks had gotten wet and his feet were extremely cold in those wet socks. Even though the cabin was not in good condition with its sagging ceiling and evidence that rodents and other animals had been in it chewing up things, they started a fire in the cabin and quickly warmed up. It was a wonderful place to sleep on that cold night.

Proceeding on down the Fortymile, they came to a narrow part of the river. The dads wanted to run the rapids there but the women and children were to walk the shoreline and be picked up on the other end. Bill was happy with this arrangement, but Al and Ben insisted that Bill join the men in the raft and brave the rapids. It took some convincing, but after it was all over, Bill was glad he had done it. Although he was nervous about the whole escapade with its intimidating big rocks and white water, in the end it was truly exciting and made another great memory.

The next morning started out as a regular day of fishing off the sides of the raft, battling the hordes of mosquitoes and other insects, so quiet, one could literally feel the silence. There was no drone of engines, no rush of traffic, no honking horns, no shouts or murmurs of human voices, no hum of electricity-driven appliances and devices. In this quiet of nature, they saw wildlife in its natural habitat, caught some fish, and eventually floated into the Yukon River. The Yukon, more than 2000 miles long, starts in the Canadian subarctic and follows a northwesterly course, crossing the entire state of Alaska, its gigantic delta emptying into the Bering Sea.

They pulled into Jack Wade, an old gold mining camp on Wade Creek, about 46 miles south of Eagle near the Alaska/Canada border. They approached an old man who was outside his cabin, and discovered he was a gold miner, still working this claim. When Al heard this, he started negotiating with the miner to purchase a nugget. Inside the cabin, one wall was literally lined with jelly jars full of gold nuggets, maybe 50-100 jars, right in full view. The visitors concluded that this place was so remote, accessible only by small boats, that there was little fear of getting robbed. After some negotiating, Al managed to purchase an ounce of gold nuggets, paying $175 cash. Seeing all this gold in the middle of the wilderness was an unforgettable sight.

The visitors walked down to the area where the old timer was still placer mining. High-pressure jets of water were used to dislodge the dirt and rocks from the sides of the mountain where it was then put through sluice boxes. There the dirt was washed away and the heavier gold settled out. This hydraulic mining is a much faster way to find gold than using a gold pan, but it destroys the land. Young Bill was excited to see real miners mining for gold, but he did not approve of the way they did it.

Continuing down the Yukon, they saw Natives fishing with fish traps, and were invited to eat some of their smoked salmon. Bill reflected that just two years before this, he had been attending school in California with child actors and famous people's kids. Now he was the kid who could claim he had floated down the mighty Yukon River. How many kids can make that claim?

CHAPTER 10

SOURDOUGH: THE MOVIE

From 1974-1977 while they were living in Anchorage with their first two children, managing apartment buildings and other enterprises, Al challenged himself with yet another project that he had no experience in. Perhaps it was a kind of preparation for their own move to the Arctic in a few years, not realizing that was even a possibility at the time. This project became a huge learning process in his life as an entrepreneur.

One day, Gil Perry, a 70-year-old man, walked into Bob Pendleton's advertising business in Anchorage with a box full of 16 mm film about his life in a remote section of the Brooks Range, a 700-miles-long-range running east to west, above the Arctic Circle. The films documented Gil's experiences, from when he left the crowded lifestyle of Anchorage and took up residence in the remote Brooks Range. Disgusted with life in the city, he chose to live off the grid in the remote Arctic for ten years. While living this rugged lifestyle, he photographed the events that shaped his life during those years. Using a 16 mm camera, he captured the wild beauty and rugged lifestyle he lived that eventually became a full-blown 35 mm movie with Gil as the main character. This movie eventually played in theaters throughout the United States.

After meeting Gil Perry, Al and his friend Bob agreed to fill in the empty parts of his life experiences by shooting additional footage to make his story complete. A log raft was built, held together with wire and bungee cords, that would carry 70-year-old Gil and his two big dogs down Six Mile Creek. This is a challenging river with class four and five rapids on the Kenai Peninsula. Cameras were positioned at various locations along the river to photograph the raft as it went plunging through the rapids. This segment became a major part of the movie.

During the ten years Gil was in the Brooks Range, he became very close to the wildlife near his cabin, even to the point of building somewhat of a relationship with some of them. Over the years his friendship with a band of Dall sheep enabled him to get some unusual photographs of himself with his arms around one of the sheep's necks. Needing some fall colors to fit the background for the movie, the film crew went up to Denali National Park to shoot the beautiful fall colors. While filming, a large grizzly charged a bull caribou that was feeding on the tundra. The caribou, rather than running away from the bear, charged the grizzly and engaged in a battle that lasted several minutes before the grizzly was able to overcome it. This encounter would later fill eight pages of a *National Geographic Magazine*. This segment also became a prominent part of the movie trailer.

Upon completing the production of the movie, Al and Bob began trying to market the film. Having very little money for this, but having lots of creativity and entrepreneurial drive, they came up with the idea of "four walling" the film. This means they went into a city in Alaska, bought television ads to broadcast the trailer of the film, rented an auditorium, and then showed the movie to audiences that were intrigued by the trailer. The first week, they filled the auditorium every night. They thought they might be able to have similar success without the expense of advertising on television but discovered attendance was cut dramatically without the ads.

After "four walling" the movie for several weeks, they were able to approach theaters to show the movie who were now interested after seeing its success. They found a group of investors to manage the affairs with Martin Spinelli the leader of this group. By this time, Al had learned enough to know that he would realize very little financial gain. It wasn't until three years later when he sold his interest in the movie that he finally made some profit from the project. The film went on to do quite well and can still be watched on streaming services.

CHAPTER 11

———◆·◆·◆———

ANAKTUVUK PASS
LIFE AMONG THE NUNAMIUT,
WHERE THE CARIBOU POOP
1979-1981

In the early days, right before and after statehood (1959), the population of Alaska was less than 200,000. No reservations were set up for the Natives in Alaska as they had been for the Natives in the lower 48. It was fortunate that the government had learned from their mistakes in how they handled the Indians in the lower 48. In Alaska Native corporations were set up so that only the State of Alaska and the Native people own the mineral rights to the land. These Native corporations were an important part of the Thompson story in Anaktuvuk Pass and Wainwright.

With the bankruptcy taking nearly all their resources, they were thankful when friends loaned them the money to go to California to take classes to get their teaching certificates renewed in the fall of 1979. An old co-worker friend of Connie's was the superintendent of schools of the enormous North Slope Borough School District.

They applied and were hired on the spot, accepting teaching positions at Anaktuvuk Pass, a relatively new village settled by people who had lived and thrived for centuries in this frozen treeless part of the state. It is now inside the boundary of the Gates of the Arctic National Park, 63 miles above the Arctic Circle. When they arrived on January 1, 1980, Anaktuvuk Pass was a village of only 175 people, who were living a life dramatically different from the way of life the people had once led as nomads between Canada and Alaska. In fact, even though these nomadic people have lived in this area for over 4000 years, they had only been discovered twenty years before the Thompsons arrived there to teach.

Early Nunamiut Life

In the old days the Nunamiut, mountain Eskimos, depended on dog sleds for transportation and followed the caribou herds. They built traditional temporary homes made of caribou hides stretched over willow frames with a caribou hide floor, similar to Mandan lodges, erected in a valley near where the caribou herd was. A more permanent structure would be a sod house built from tundra blocks, the window made of grizzly intestines. They would return to this home after hunting season was over. Food consisted entirely of caribou meat and an occasional fish, wild blueberries and squawberries. For centuries these people were so isolated in their village that they rarely saw other people except for when they would travel to trade furs to whaling captains for needed goods.

The Thompson's Native friend, Bob Ahgook, shared some history of the area with them. The early people often developed scurvy because their diet of caribou and more caribou (members of the deer family) did not provide all the nutrients needed. The solution was that in the spring of the year they would go out and watch the herd grazing on the tundra. After about an hour, one caribou was shot, the contents of its first stomach were removed and put into hot water where they let it set for an hour. The people would drink the fluid, and this would provide the vitamins needed to prevent scurvy. It is hard to imagine how, through the course of history, they were able to come up with this remedy.

When Europeans arrived, the Presbyterians built a log church in the village. This was no small feat as there are no trees growing in the area. Logs had to be cut and hauled for quite a distance. Many people in the village attended church and accepted Christianity. Al thinks the people were so close to nature that they realized there had to be a greater power in the world.

In 1961 the Nunamiuts settled down at the top of a wide 2100-foot mountain pass through which 28,000 to 30,000 caribou passed on their way to the calving grounds twice a year. The pass is known as Anaktuvuk Pass which literally means "the place where the caribou poop." Only seven years later, in March 1968, oil was discovered on the North Slope.

The Anaktuvuk people shared in the mineral rights and became extremely wealthy. This wealth propelled them rapidly into the 20th century with modern homes and conveniences they had known nothing about not so many years before.

Anaktuvuk Pass

Tuniks Arrive on the North Slope

In the middle of the winter of 1980, Al, Connie, Michael (who was just a baby), and their daughter left Anchorage on an Alaska Airlines jet bound for Fairbanks, then transferred to a smaller plane for the 250-mile flight north into the middle of the Brooks Range in the Arctic. Connie remembers that this felt like the beginning of the life that God had planned for them all along. They witnessed what they thought was the most beautiful scenery of any in the world, traveling through dangerous mountain passes and a long valley with a spectacular mountain range on both sides.

There were no cars in the village of Anaktuvuk Pass so they were met at the runway with snow machines pulling sleds behind to transport them and their luggage to what was to be their new home for the next year and a half. The Thompsons, dressed in down parkas and snow pants, brought a beautiful sled dog with them. While unloading the dog from the airplane, the local people yelled out, "*Tunik* has dog!"--"White man has dog!" The dog immediately impacted their relationships, creating friends in the village. Not only the sled dog but also Al's science background enriched their experiences in the village. Some of their experiences involved being out in the field with the Native people and experiencing their lifestyle with the caribou, still central to their lifestyle regardless of the impact of 20th century civilization.

The bankruptcy had taken their beautiful spacious home on the Anchorage Hillside only a few months before and they now moved into a small triplex. This small but modern home, just like those of the Natives, had a kitchen, two bedrooms, a bathroom and a porch–but no well, even though there was plumbing in the house. Water had to be hauled to the house, and put into two 100-gallon tanks for use, accessible with the faucets in the kitchen and bathroom.

Their toilet was a "honey bucket," as they were called in "the bush," the remote areas of Alaska that are not on the road or ferry system. This five-gallon can with a toilet seat and a heavy-duty plastic sack insert had to be taken outdoors to be dumped into a special area where it would freeze during the winter. In the spring after the thaw, it was taken out with a loader and dumped into the ocean.

Besides a considerable downsizing of their living space, they exchanged their view of Anchorage, Cook Inlet, and Denali (known as Mt. McKinley in those days) for a view of the Arctic National Wildlife Preserve and a front row seat to the caribou migration that went right through this small village.

Life in this cold environment presented many challenges. Even though they had a dog, they did not have a sled to pull Michael, so he was transported on Connie's back, tucked under her Eddie Bauer coat. One bitterly cold morning, when they arrived at the babysitter, Connie saw that Michael had a quarter-sized white circle on one of his cheeks–frostbite! This reminded Connie of the 30-30-30 factor. If the wind is blowing 30 miles an hour and it's 30 degrees below zero, bare skin will freeze in 30 seconds.

They learned to be as excited as the Natives when the small airplane flew into the village three times a week carrying much anticipated mail, packages of food and other items ordered by the residents–if the weather permitted. When an approaching plane was heard, everyone in the village went running out to the airport on the edge of town.

Airplanes were an important link to the world outside their isolated environment. When a person was experiencing a medical emergency, it was an airplane that came to take him to medical facilities outside the village. If it was dark when the plane came, everyone hurried to the airport with their snow machines to light the runway with their headlights for the plane to land safely.

Their daughter, a freshman, attended school here for one semester, but being the only non-Eskimo student in the high school was too much of a challenge for her. She had already faced so many changes in the few short years since she joined the family that she chose to stay home with Michael and be homeschooled for a semester. Since they had no home in Anchorage any longer, they spent the summer months in Hawaii. After that first summer, their daughter decided she did not want to go back to Anaktuvuk Pass. Instead, she went to live with Connie's sister in California and eventually graduated from high school in California.

Adapting to the 20th Century

When the Thompsons arrived in Anaktuvuk Pass that winter, the village was already trying to adapt to the new ways of life in the 20th Century. The village's one telephone, shared by everyone, was located in the corner of the one and only small store. A brand new modern public school had been built with oil money, on stilts eight feet above the ground, complete with a swimming pool, a gym with a polished wooden floor, and a well-stocked library. What they did not have were cars, televisions, or flush toilets.

The swimming pool became an example of how people tend to cling to their old ways. These people never before had the opportunity, need, or desire to go swimming. There was no place to swim in this frigid climate. Instead, the pool became a reservoir for fighting fires. Eventually the younger people did use it for swimming, but the older people never did as they just could not adapt to the new and crazy idea of immersing themselves into water.

Another portion of the village's newfound wealth paid the way for any families with children to go to Hawaii for two years and attend school there if they chose to do so. Shortly before the Thompsons arrived, the families with children had all returned. What an adjustment that had to be going from Alaska to Hawaii and back again. This was more evidence of how wealthy the village had become with the discovery of oil!

Besides the multi-million-dollar school, a modern airport was built and the small village store provided new and different food. The lifestyle of these nomadic mountain Eskimos went from living in tundra sod houses and caribou lodges to settling into modern 3-bedroom houses, using snow machines for transportation rather than dog teams, and eating modern foods they had not hunted and killed themselves.

Al became friends with several Natives, notably Johnny Ruhland, Bob Ahgook, and Roosevelt Panaik. When Al visited one of his Native friends in his home, all his belongings were on the floor, spread out around him where he could see them. The Native was used to being able to see all his possessions and had difficulty adjusting to the modern way of putting things away on shelves and in closets and cupboards.

Johnny demonstrated the hardiness of the people by often repairing his snow machine in the frigid -25 degrees temperatures, dressed in a t-shirt, for hours on end. Bob demonstrated his knowledge of the tundra by showing Al how the wolves lived in this area. They would often go out to a wolf den and wait for the mother to leave the den looking for food. They would go down to the den, Bob would reach in and pull two cubs out at a time and have his picture taken with them. Roosevelt and Al were observing the behavior of a black wolf in the wolf clan. When it was time for the men to eat, Al ate a peanut butter sandwich Connie had packed for him, but Roosevelt took out a shinbone of a caribou, split it in half, took his knife, peeled the marrow out of the bone, spread it on a slice of bread and ate it. Protein is protein but Al could not bring himself to try it. This kind of diet made the Natives physically strong.

On another memorable day, Johnny knocked on Al's door and asked him how many bullets he had. Al had about five boxes of 270 rifle ammunition. When he heard this news, Johnny said, "You will be the shooter. Come with me!"

There were 107 caribou that had been trapped in the Fourth of July Canyon. The men went to the head of the canyon and, two by two, the Natives drove caribou out of the canyon. In about an hour, Al had shot all 107 caribou, the summer meat supply for the village. The gun was fired so many times that the stock was charred from the heat of it.

The Native women came out and joyfully butchered the caribou. The carcasses were loaded onto a pole through a hole right under the caribou's jaw. These were then dragged to the village over the crusted snow by a snow machine, five at a time. There the meat was lowered into a permafrost freezer, a four foot by six foot, 25-foot deep shaft, dug into the ground. A whole caribou could be lowered into the shaft all at once. Once the bottom of the shaft was reached, the caribou was hung in a five foot by seven-foot tunnel that was about 50 feet long. The meat would stay frozen all summer in this natural freezer. The average family of four would consume over 35 caribou per year so that many were needed to feed the village.

The Old Meets New

One day Al was teaching when a student came in and wanted permission to leave for a couple of weeks. She was going on a snow machine trip over 80 miles away that would take about 4 days to complete. The temperature was a bone-chilling -45 degrees. All their gear was on a dogsled, towed by the snow machine for this extremely cold journey. This was another example of the mixing of the old and new and the Native ability to survive in this harsh environment.

Another day Al was unloading a dog food shipment at the airport. Roosevelt was surprised by this and wondered why

Al didn't just feed the dogs caribou. The next day they took off on a snowmachine and shot two caribou. Once a month, they would repeat this, and the dogs were perfectly content chewing on caribou carcasses until nothing was left but the bones. The skeletons needed to be removed to the dump (another new thing) as the village no longer moved from place to place and had to deal with waste disposal.

The school's principal was well respected in the village. He was an asset to all as he would provide after-hours classes at the school specifically for the Native adults. Knife-making was a popular class taught by him and some of the Natives. He was able to get good iron and steel that was not otherwise available to the Natives. Leather working was another popular class. These classes helped build a great relationship with parents who had to trust the school system with their children.

The Thompsons stayed here for only a year and half, and it was with sorrow that this was such a short sojourn. Al enjoyed teaching at the high school, and Connie enjoyed a semester of teaching junior high, and a year of teaching third grade. They identified with the struggles of the people and were fascinated by their history. They became people with whom they had developed close ties. They would have stayed longer, but the North Slope Borough School District superintendent knew of Al's entrepreneurial experience and urged them to consider a move to Wainwright, another school on the North Slope, so that he could use his skills to help with the developing Native corporations.

CHAPTER 12

WAINWRIGHT 1981-1989

In the fall of 1981, Connie, Al, and their young son Michael moved to the village of Wainwright (different from Fort Wainwright near Fairbanks where Al taught when they moved to Alaska in 1961) to teach first grade and biology. With no roads to this isolated bush village, a flight to Barrow, then a transfer to a second smaller plane designed to land on a short gravel runway was required to reach Wainwright.

Wainwright was a traditional whaling village of about 400 Inupiat Eskimos at this time, 90 miles west of Point Barrow on the Arctic Ocean. In this extreme northern location, only about 800 miles from the North Pole, the sun does not come above the horizon for almost three months in the winter. They learned to dress more like the Natives, donning snow pants and fur-trimmed parkas with not an inch of flesh exposed that did not have to be. Their Native women friends helped trim their Eddie Bauer outerwear with wolf and Arctic fox fur ruffs around the edge of the hoods. When these thick fur ruffs were pulled out around their faces, they would help warm the air before it was inhaled and also helped protect their faces from frostbite.

Allen and Michael at Wainwright in their Arctic gear. Photo credit: Allen Thompson

The months-long Arctic darkness and cold climate were truly a challenge, a source of much depression among those who have to live in it although the Natives did not seem to be affected by the long periods of darkness as much as the non-Natives. They tried to focus on learning the traditions of this Native culture, teaching the Eskimo children, and getting to know and love these people of the far North. Their son, Michael, was a source of strength and joy during these years.

Their house in Wainwright was modern and adequate for their needs, very similar to their house at Anaktuvuk Pass within walking distance of the school. However, water was an even bigger challenge here than in Anaktuvuk Pass. Wells could not be drilled here because one would have to go through several hundred feet of permafrost to reach water, and then pipes would freeze making it impossible to pump the water out. In addition, the water here was too acidic to drink. The school's principal made sure all of the teachers had a water distiller for their use or else he would have had a faculty that was very ill! They bathed only once a week as water was always rationed by the village.

Rather than getting water delivered twice a week and put into their 100-gallon tanks as they did at Anaktuvuk Pass, the whole community harvested large blocks of ice, cutting them out of a nearby lake with large saws about six to seven feet long with very large teeth. The large blocks of ice were placed on ice tables outside of the houses. From the end of September to the middle of May, there was always a block of ice on these tables available to thaw.

When the water in the storage tank was running low, a chunk of ice would be added to the tank. To speed up the melting process, a pump would be turned on to circulate water around the ice, so that they always had an ample supply of drinking water.

Ice harvest. Photo credit: Dave Finley

The ice pile at the lake. Photo credit: Dave Finley

Whaling, an Essential Eskimo Endeavor

The Thompsons were able to witness the vital village tradition of hunting bowhead whales. Every spring, whaling crews launched their umiaqs, boats made of bearded seal skins stretched over a wood frame, into the icy blue waters of the Arctic Ocean in search of the whales. Every village on the North Slope is allowed to kill a small number of bowhead whales each year for their subsistence. Besides being the traditional food and source of other vital resources they had depended on for generations, food from outside is so expensive that whale meat is an essential part of the diet for all Eskimo people. Whale meat is below a layer of maktak (the rubbery black outer skin of the whale with a layer of blubber beneath the skin, about 12-18 inches thick, eaten raw), rich in omega 3 oils and protein.

While the Thompsons were living there, the Eskimos still hunted and harvested whales in the traditional ways. A whaling crew consisted of an umiaq, a captain, and eight to ten young men who provided the rowing power for the boat. The captain sat in the rear of the umiaq, steering the vessel into position either to the left or the right of the wake created by the whale's swimming motions to allow the optimal positioning for a clear shot. The harpooner would be in the very front of the boat, the designated weapon shooter. When the umiaq was close enough to the whale and in good position, the harpooner would fire the harpoon into the lung of the whale, ensuring its death.

Once the whale was killed out in the ocean, all 50-70 tons of the kill had to be towed to the edge of the Arctic ice, about 25-30 miles from the actual edge of the land. Getting the whale to the edge of the ice shore was a great chore, but then the entire village showed up and used the muscle power of hundreds of people, heavy ropes and block and tackle to lift the heavy whale onto the ice. This task often took a whole day of pulling, moving the great hulk inch by inch.

A whale on the ice, ready for processing at Wainwright.
Photo credit: Allen Thompson

Then the butchering process began. Tradition dictates that the prized pieces of the whale, the dorsal fins, be given to the captain. This apparent delicacy was eaten raw by the captain and his family, a high honor. The other parts of the whale were cut up, the elders given second choice of whale meat portions, and the rest of the village shared the remainder. Two whales provide enough protein for the entire village for one full year.

Bowhead whales are baleen whales, filter feeders. They have massive thick skulls that help them to break through the thick ice. Inside their enormous heads, rather than teeth they have long baleen plates that hang from their upper jaw, similar to the teeth of a comb, with long hairs on the inside edge. These plates are made of keratin, the same substance as human hair and fingernails. When the whale feeds, it will suck in thousands of gallons of ocean water while it is under water, then expel it through these plates. The hair-like inner edges of these hundreds of plates capture their food, where their several-ton tongue will swipe over the "hairs" and the food is swallowed whole.

Natives harvest the baleen plates from the whales and use them in many ways. Over the centuries, the hair-like fibers have been used like string to tie harpoon tips to the shaft and to make fish lines and nets. Baskets have been made from baleen and still are today. Strong and flexible, baleen can be cut and polished or engraved with scrimshaw art.

The Natives also enjoyed mikigaq, whale meat that has been cut into long two-inch strips, placed into a five-gallon bucket, covered with whale blood, and allowed to ferment for several months until the meat is tender enough to be cut with a fork. Although considered to be an Inupiaq delicacy, Al says you do not want to be downwind when they open that bucket.

The bones and entrails were left to be scavenged by the numerous polar bears that would show up to join in the Arctic whaling celebration. These white bears would turn black for a short time from rolling in the greasy fat of the whale residue, embedding it into their fur. This "styling gel" plastered their translucent fur to their skin so that their skin showed through, black as charcoal. Thus, for a short period of time, there were some "black bears" in the Arctic.

A recent event in the Arctic solved a riddle with a long-hidden answer regarding the longevity of the bowhead whale. It once was a common belief that bowhead whales had a life span about equal to a human's. Although research is still being conducted, new evidence contradicts this belief. For example, a 71-foot-long bowhead killed at Barter Island was found to have a washtub-sized gristle formation surrounding an ivory harpoon that had been embedded near the whale's lungs. Village elders said that type of harpoon was last used in the 1800s by Eskimo hunters. This discovery led them to conclude that the whale was over 220 years old. In addition to this discovery, stone harpoon spear tips have been found embedded in whales harvested in recent years.

This find led to the ability to identify the age of all bowhead whales when killed. They are believed to be the oldest mammals on the planet, their longevity attributed to their environment. There is no food in the Arctic Ocean for the whale to feed on for 6 months of the year, the water temperature is an average of 35 degrees year-round, and the bowhead does not migrate to warmer waters. In fact, bowhead whales can go without eating for more than a year, surviving on their immense reserve of stored fat. Apparently, this combination of factors enables such a long life.

Because of his background in biology, one summer Al did research with the Alaska Eskimo Whaling Commission collecting pathogens that affected the bowhead whale's magnetic sense of navigation. Whales have an incredible amount of magnetic material in their brains, but the microscopic pathogens in the brains of the whales cause them to get disoriented and beach themselves. Information Al collected from these beached whales ultimately made its way to the International Whaling Commission in London. This information was used to further their scientific understanding of the behavior of bowhead whales.

Eskimo Endurance and Inevitable Change

An unusual characteristic of Eskimos is their ability to endure their cold Arctic environment. From October to March the temperatures average between +18 degrees and -18 degrees with lows sometimes reaching -56 degrees. The "hottest" month, July, has an average high of 52 degrees and low of 39 degrees. The sun rises in mid-May and does not set again until the end of July, providing light for long summer days. The long winter night begins when the sun sets around

November 21, and does not rise above the horizon again until about January 20.

The tradition of eating raw meat and very few vegetables has enabled the Eskimos to adapt to this harsh environment and to live here successfully for centuries. Most Eskimos have a layer of fat below their skin that helps them endure their harsh environment. Their short stature helps conserve body heat and enables them to withstand the cold.

Because of the oil discovery in the Arctic and the arrival of communication technologies such as the telephone and television, a new way of life suddenly exploded into the Wainwright subsistence lifestyle, just as it had in Anaktuvuk Pass. Besides more communication with life "outside," the rapid accumulation of oil money brought more than just modern housing and the use of snow machines rather than traditional dog teams. It might seem like a small thing compared to all the other changes facing these people, but one significant change was how they got food.

Traditional hunting no longer supplied all the food needed by the Natives of the village partly because of new regulations imposed on them and partly because of the influx of non-Natives who created a demand for food not usually eaten in this part of the Arctic. The majority of groceries were ordered a year in advance and delivered by barge. These extreme northern waters are only navigable for about 45 days a year necessitating careful advance planning. Supply orders would be written out, and one of the teachers would travel to Seattle to do the shopping. Supplies were then loaded onto a Bureau of Land Management ship that took the items from Seattle to Nome. At Nome, they were loaded onto the Northwind, an ocean-going landing craft ship. This ship would stop at all the major Arctic villages to unload grocery orders.

Some preferred to order groceries weekly or monthly, this food flown in from Fairbanks. Although this method of shopping was much more expensive, it was used by the people who survived on whale and other local meats in the old subsistence tradition. Whenever anyone left the village to go to Fairbanks, they would take a list of everyone's needs to purchase when there. In the years while the Thompsons were living in the Arctic, fresh items such as milk ($10 a gallon) and vegetables would be purchased in this way. Cabbage, carrots and beets were the only fresh vegetables that would last long periods of time without refrigeration.

Each house had a separate storage pantry built onto the house designed to store groceries. Part of the Thompson annual order always included fifty-six 24-packs of Diet Coke. Storage of this many cases of liquid required some creativity resulting in Diet Coke stashes all over the house—in closets, under the bed, and in every available nook. One year while they were gone to Hawaii for Christmas, the electricity went out, the soda froze and exploded, making a mess that took a long time to clean up!

Another major change was that the education of young children became more of a possibility as well as a high priority. Seven brand new modern schools, one per village, were built in the North Slope Borough School District, the largest landmass area school district in the United States—94,000 square miles of sparsely inhabited area. According to 2023 statistics found on the North Slope Borough website, only 2,058 students are enrolled in prekindergarten through grade 12. The schools became responsible for bringing 20th century life to an extremely remote subsistence culture. (https://www.niche.com/k12/d/north-slope-borough-school-district-ak/)

The transition from subsistence to the great wealth and capitalism of the oil boom affected nearly everything on a daily basis and was very difficult for the Eskimo people to adapt to. Alcoholism became a huge problem because of this rapid transition.

A Zoo for Mr. Thompson

Wainwright was a culture that historically had no need for formal education. What the Lower 48 would consider the necessary "reading, writing, and 'rithmetic" was not valued nor encouraged. The transition that catapulted the Eskimos into a capitalist world demanded that they become concerned with these subjects—and quickly! But that didn't mean that the parents or students necessarily saw this need. It was essential to figure out a way to get the students to *want* to be in school, to motivate them to participate and learn.

Curiosity is a gateway to learning, and most people seem to be interested in animals. Eskimos had been a subsistence culture for thousands of years and they knew a lot about the animals that lived in their environment. In this culture, the people who were considered to be successful were the skilled hunters. Whaling captains had the highest status in the Eskimo culture. Their knowledge of the bowhead whale and how to hunt and kill them was key to being a successful whale hunter.

Once again, Al's biology background became the source of inspiration. He introduced animals that were not a part of the Alaskan fauna to get and hold their attention, setting up what came to be known as "Al's Zoo." He used these animals to get kids to pay attention and motivate them to be present in school. The school district had a good supply of money to do what he wanted to do, so with great enthusiasm and inspiration, he set up a successful program that included activities and animals that the whole community wanted to come to witness.

Al's classroom zoo started with two ferrets, Jumper and Whistler. These friendly, playful and curious animals quickly gained the affection of the students with their antics. Students would learn facts about the ferrets as they played with them, recorded their observations, and took turns supervising their care and feeding. They were able to compare the animals of this family to others that they were already familiar with—weasels and minks. The students bonded with Jumper and Whistler and wanted to come to school to interact with them.

What soon became a classroom and community favorite was Julius Squeezer, a 24-inch boa constrictor. This animal was totally out of the realm of their understanding as there are no snakes living in Alaska. Individual students were assigned to handle and care for the snake. Over a period of many months the snake even became familiar with and would welcome the students. One day Al was surprised when a student in his computer class was busily typing with Julius Squeezer wrapped around her neck.

Boa constrictor feeding time became a community attraction. His lunch, a live white mouse, was released into Julius Squeezer's cage, Julius would mesmerize the mouse, then strike with his fangs and wrap his body around the mouse, squeezing the air out of it until it died. Then he would slowly swallow the mouse while everyone watched. They were fascinated to see the big lump traveling down the length of the snake's body as the mouse was digested. Although the non-Eskimo culture might think this lesson was a bit barbaric, Eskimos are as used to dealing with the death of animals as they are used to the necessity of killing animals for food.

Another popular critter was Tommy the Tarantula. He looked very frightening to the students but after Al demonstrated how Tommy would eat crickets, they enjoyed feeding Tommy as well. Tarantulas surround the cricket with their body and legs, crouch over their prey and snatch it with their mouth. Eventually the kids would put the cricket on their hands and let Tommy walk across their skin, over the cricket, and watch him snatch it up into his mouth. Even adults were fascinated with this giant spider.

Besides these unusual specimens, Al's zoo also had frogs, fish and birds. They were all available for the students to help care for and learn from. The animals were a reason kids wanted to come to school, an important motivation to be where they needed to be to learn. Often Al would assign an hour's worth of homework so that the kids could complete it outside the classroom and have more time to play with the animals during the school day. At night, even the custodians would come to Al's room to watch the animals.

More Motivation for Student Success

Dave Finley, the school principal also had creative ideas for motivating students to be present and to have a good attitude. He created the "Good Attitude Lounge," a place where students could play various video games, eat free food, and relax. In order to gain access to this special space, the students had to have accumulated "Good Attitude Passes" which were given out by teachers in their classes. The students had to pay attention and not use bad language.

This popular incentive helped greatly with student behavior and even helped improve student grades.

An Unwelcome Polar Bear Visitor

One animal that is familiar to the residents of Wainwright is the polar bear, the planet's largest land predator. These huge Arctic animals can weigh 1700 pounds and measure eight feet long. They are built for warmth with hollow white fur that insulates and reflects light, providing camouflage in their snowy environment. Beneath their black skin is a thick layer of fat that further insulates them from the cold air and water where they spend time hunting and capturing their favorite meal–seals! Their huge paws help distribute their weight on the ice and have non-slip pads for better control in their slippery environment. Biologists classify polar bears as marine mammals since most of their time is spent in the icy water. They only need land for breeding and do not hibernate as their food source is available all year long.

Polar bears are also a danger to humans in this environment that is the bears' home. So, one day, when one polar bear, perhaps an older bear that had lost its strength and was looking for something to eat, came wandering into town, it was not a welcome visitor. The village was only about 500 yards from the ice pack of the Arctic Ocean. The bear came down from the water, made a right turn onto a neighborhood street, and began his journey, but not unnoticed. Fortunately, a man spotted the bear early on and got onto his CB radio, calling a neighbor down the street to alert him of the bear's arrival. The bear was headed right toward a group of children who were playing outside on their bicycles, including Al and Connie's son, Michael.

The forewarned citizen grabbed his gun, ran out of his house, and took down the bear, killing it with only one shot. It is quite unusual to kill a bear of this size with only one shot!

Although polar bear meat is extremely high in protein, it is inedible because of its strong unpleasant flavor. Even though the meat is unusable, the hide is a precious commodity. They quickly skinned the bear and used the hide, its thick fur making a wonderfully warm coat or rug.

When the bear was dead, the children all gathered around this magnificent beast. It was a memorable event in this remote village!

Michael and the polar bear. Photo credit Allen Thompson

Sunken Ship

Many interesting things happened during these Wainwright years. One notable event happened early one winter morning when Barry Bodfish called Al and told him to come to the beach. The night before, a strong storm had hit Wainwright and exposed the remains of a large clipper ship that had run aground on a sandbar in the Bay way back in the 1800s. Part of a large multi-ship whaling expedition, it had been stranded in the ice near the whaling village of present-day Barter Island. The purpose of that expedition had been to hunt bowhead whales for their whale oil and baleen. Baleen was used by the garment industry in those days to make female girdles and bras.

After being locked into the ice for 1.5 years, the ships made a run for the Pacific Ocean. As fate would have it, the flotilla made it only as far as Wainwright Bay, some 600 miles from Barter Island. The ice closed in on the flotilla once again, jacked the ships up onto the ice, tipped them over, and spilled their contents into the Bay. All of the ships eventually sank into the Bay but there were no fatalities. The crew was able to evacuate to the village of Wainwright, hauling out their cargo with hopes to retrieve it at a later time.

Barry and Al walked out to the sandbar, climbed into the ship and found a brass plate indicating this was a steam-powered clipper ship, built in Boston, Massachusetts, in 1836. The ship was constructed with dowels and brass spikes. Al removed a portion of the ship held together by wooden dowels and donated it to the Museum of the North in Barrow, Alaska. Al deeply regrets that he did not have a camera to document this experience.

Artifact from the 1800s whaling ship

Barry said that the last time this ship had been visible was when he was six years old, 51 years earlier. On the day that Barry and Al saw it, it was above water for about six to eight hours and hasn't been seen since then. It would take just the right tide and just the right storm to expose it again—unless the shifting sands have consigned it to the deep forever. Only time will tell.

The Permafrost Problem

The ground on the North Slope is made up of permafrost that can extend from 500 to 2000 feet below the surface. The top one to three feet of permafrost, the "active layer," thaws during the summer as the weather warms. Additionally, the heat from anything built on top of permafrost causes greater thawing. Typically, a structure built on permafrost will settle and tilt, just as Al and Connie's homestead cabin near Fairbanks did. According to the experts, it is best to avoid building anything on permafrost.

However, once the wealth of the oil fields came to the North Slope and the lifestyles changed from subsistence to capitalism, buildings became necessary as did finding ways to mitigate the damage thawing permafrost would inflict on the homes, schools, and businesses that needed to be built.

Science and engineering have come up with ingenious ways of building on permafrost. The schools on the North Slope had to be built on pilings, raising them eight feet off the ground to allow cold air to circulate beneath the structure which helps protect the permafrost from thawing from the heat of the building. When a structure cannot be raised, then a simple device known as a thermosyphon is embedded into the permafrost. These use natural refrigerant gasses to remove the heat from the permafrost and help to protect it from thawing. (source: https://www.conocophillips.com/sustainability/sustainability-news/story/using-thermosyphons-on-alaska-s-north-slope/)

These schools cost millions of dollars to build due their remote locations and the challenges of building a school on permafrost. Just the 100 flush toilets in Barrow cost about a million dollars each as thermosyphons had to be used to prevent thawing of the permafrost.

School on Fire!

The elementary school at Wainwright had eight classrooms, and the high school had six with an enrollment of about 55. The two schools were connected by a long heated and carpeted hallway with large windows on both sides. The school was an important part of the community with a gymnasium that was a popular place for many to gather in the evenings for an informal game of basketball or other physical activity. One early November evening was going to rapidly and tragically change the community.

It all started when two kids with burning sticks were pretending to be sword fighting underneath the school. Normally children would not have access to this space, but someone had left the gate open that gave them access to this large area. While the kids were playing, the insulation under the gym floor caught fire. The people in the gym felt the heat through the floor, so hot that they started to question what was going on. They immediately called the maintenance man for help and evacuated the building.

It was not long before the school custodian pounded on the Thompsons' door and reported that the high school was on fire. He, Barry Bodfish and Al ran up to the school, went around the back side and tried to open the kitchen door. It was so hot they could barely touch it, and they soon realized how foolish it would be to open that door. They quickly abandoned that plan and tried to figure out what to do in this remote area where there was no such thing as a fire department or fire trucks to call for help.

Barry feared the whole school complex would go up in flames and Al wondered if there was a way to isolate the high school from the elementary school to prevent that from happening. Then Barry remembered a school fire at another village school a few years before and how they managed to confine that fire.

Barry quickly got a D-8 Caterpillar and tilted the blade up quite high to reach the structure that was eight feet above the ground. He managed to maneuver in such a way as to avoid the structure falling on top of him while he rammed the Cat through the connecting structure. Amid the loud crunching of the Cat blade crashing into the building and the shattering of glass, Barry struck the building with all the force he could get out of the machine.

The first run hit the wall of the structure right where there were many electrical wires. The severed wires shot out a large shower of electrical fireballs and sparks that bounced off the Cat for several seconds while Barry was inside. It was more than fortunate that Barry had on thick gloves that helped to insulate his hands from the electrical charge traveling through the metal parts of the Cat. Al was surprised that

Barry was not harmed at all as it appeared certain that he would have been burned at the least or electrocuted at worst.

Barry crashed into the structure several more times until he had succeeded in isolating the burning high school from the elementary school. Although the operation was a success as it did save the elementary school, the fire caused a great loss to the community. That night they lost the high school, administrative offices, gym, kitchen, and electrical generating plant that provided power for the whole village. The only thing the people could do was stand and watch the destruction as these structures burned to the ground.

With no electrical power to run pumps, the swimming pool water reservoir was useless. The whole village was without power for about two days in the cold. The State of Alaska flew in an emergency power plant to provide electricity for the village, one of seven or eight generators that the State kept on hand for times such as this.

This incident made it evident that something more needed to be done to guard against another tragedy like this. In an area where there are no emergency services nearby, villages needed to be able to handle a crisis like this themselves. Within a couple of years, the village built a firehall and had two fire trucks.

The Thompsons also suffered personal losses in the fire including the destruction of all the animals in "Al's Zoo". When the superintendent in Barrow heard about the fire, she called them personally and wanted to know if the animals made it, implying that even she knew these animals had made a big impression on these kids' learning.

Another tragic result of this fire was the great loss of Al and Connie's personal property yet again. Besides all the animals that had been so valuable in Al's classroom, many of his teaching materials were destroyed. Connie lost her dad's accordion that had special meaning to her and that she enjoyed playing. Their small home did not have room for all their personal belongings, so much of it had been stored at the school.

This fire became the cause of the third time the Thompsons lost nearly everything. This third tragedy taught them that material possessions do not mean much but that their relationship and marriage was the most important thing they had, a precious commodity that fire, theft, or bankruptcy could not take away from them.

Famous Neighbor

Interesting experiences were not limited to interactions with Alaska Natives. One of the nation's best-known authors, James Michener, was writing his book, *Alaska*. In order to do his thorough research about the Eskimos, he lived in Wainwright for six months, the Thompsons' next-door neighbor. He and his wife were extremely pleasant neighbors. The Micheners often had lunch with the Thompsons in their house. His wife had a major role in helping organize her husband, but he did all the writing and research for the book. Michener gave them a signed copy of his book upon publication. It is likely that the Micheners also told their other friends about the interesting neighbors they had while living at Wainwright.

CHAPTER 13

CAPITALISM 101 FOR ALASKA NATIVES

Native Corporations

One of the major changes the Eskimo people experienced was placing them into Native corporations. Their corporate status gave Natives ownership of their land and made them responsible to the State of Alaska for financial management. The corporate status allowed them to invest their assets and provided an income for the shareholders when their corporations earned profits from their investments. Various types of investments were made by the several Native corporations, and some did very well while others were not nearly as profitable.

Student Corporations–From Big Macs to Clay Cups

It became obvious that the children needed to be educated so that they could live under this new capitalist system. While they were living at Wainwright, the teachers were charged with the responsibility of helping the children to adjust to all these rapid changes. Al had the genius idea of starting a student corporation in Wainwright to help these children understand how capitalism works. An administrative assistant to the superintendent of schools helped to carry this idea to fruition, and helped it spread to all seven schools scattered over the huge area that is the North Slope.

Since it was Al's idea, he was given the go-ahead to start a student corporation at the Wainwright high school, each student becoming a shareholder. Each of the student corporation shareholders, only 17 students in the whole high school, were given a corporate share worth $200. The student corporation established a board of directors consisting of five of the 17 students, officers to run it, and was registered with the State of Alaska to do business in the State.

At the end of their first year of operation, the Wainwright student corporation's gross income from investments from the shareholders was $80,000, earned in various ways. This was such a shocking amount that the superintendent came and audited the books. He was pleased with the results, to say the least! It was so impressive, in fact, that this model was used by the other schools in the North Slope School District to form their own student corporations.

Several different enterprises were responsible for earning all this income. One of the student Board members set up a business to sell McDonald's Big Macs flown in from Fairbanks for the weekly movie at the high school gym. In one school year, she sold over $10,000 of Big Macs at $10 each.

Another student designed and made a coffee cup featuring Arctic whales. The clay used to make the cups was harvested right out of the Arctic Ocean at Wainwright. All they had to do was shovel the clay into a bucket, and they had all they needed to make these unique cups. Over 500 were sold on the North Slope in the first year. Al traveled around Alaska marketing them and eventually bought the rights to the cup from her and renamed them "Alaska Trumpet Cups". Ultimately 42,000 of these were sold to gift shops in museums, zoos and aquariums.

After they left the Slope and lived in Indonesia, Al spent the next three summers marketing the cups in Alaska. Later he traveled to Boston, Chicago, and San Diego to sell them. Often when Al would approach a customer, they would initially show no interest in selling yet another mug in their gift shop. That is until Al opened up his sample case and showed them what he had! Then they would often be interested in this unusual cup and place an order. The most popular design was the cup with a manatee on it. Over 18,000 of these were sold by an aquarium in Florida. Al eventually sold the business to a man in Florida whom he knew when in Alaska.

After five years of operation, the student corporation at Wainwright invited all the student corporation members on the North Slope to a rock concert. A band was flown up from Anchorage ($10,000). The $60,000 tab that covered the airfare, housing and food for the more than 500 delegates from all over who attended this three-day event was all paid for by the Wainwright student corporation. This was a big thank you from the Wainwright student corporation to all of the North Slope student corporations for participating in their communities. Because of the great distances between villages, this was the first time ever that these young people had gotten together. This proved to be a great social event with benefits for the whole community as the young people were able to interact with the adults also.

In another elaborate lesson to teach how capitalism and the modern world works, Al was designated as the person to take the graduating classes, ranging from two to eight students, on a two-week trip to California to introduce them to city life. This experience introduced them to how to buy an airplane ticket and fly somewhere, order food in a restaurant, how to get a motel room while traveling, and how to catch a bus or taxi. They also went to large department stores to see how people shop, and took them to a movie theater. Every one of these experiences was so very different from anything these children had ever experienced in their lives.

CHAPTER 14

TO THE OTHER END OF THE EARTH INDONESIA–1989-1994

Even though they were eligible to retire as teachers in the State of Alaska and were ready to leave the cold environment of the North Slope, they were not ready to quit teaching. In the spring of 1989 while still teaching in Wainwright, Alaska, an appealing opportunity presented itself—a new place to teach combined with an opportunity to travel. They went to a recruitment conference and were offered very attractive jobs and an opportunity to leave footprints in yet another part of the world--Surabaya, Indonesia, a large industrial city with many factories.

They left the Arctic to teach school on the Equator, a major shift in climate, culture, customs, and values. At that time Surabaya had a population of 2.5 million. For the first time, the family was living in a foreign civilization where they were a tiny minority of less than 200 white people from the United States. Everywhere they went, they were the object of stares, touching, and conversation. It was not unusual for local people to touch, pinch, and stare at them in public because they had never seen white people before. Their son's blue eyes and blond hair were a great curiosity in this brown-eyed culture.

They lived in a lovely two-bedroom house, just Al, Connie and Michael. They were required to hire servants, and they had five for the three of them. Connie felt like she was in heaven with a servant to cook, another who did laundry by hand on the laundry patio attached to the house, another who ironed their clothes, including sheets, pillow cases, and even tee shirts and shorts! Their gardener clipped the grass on his hands and knees with a grass clipper—no lawn mower! The gardener doubled as a guard at night also. Another servant served as their driver, and another cleaned their house. If their memory is accurate, all this hired help cost only $140 a month. Everyone had servants as it was a way to provide jobs for the large population of this city.

They soon learned that this culture valued and respected teachers much more than any place they had taught in the United States. When people learned they were teachers, they would step out of line and let Al and Connie take their more advantageous place. This respect was displayed by both adults and students, and made them proud to be teachers.

The International School where Al and Connie both taught was designed for educating children from foreign nations whose parents were working for the Indonesian government and businesses. Al taught biology while Connie taught first grade, the students from 26 countries, all educated in English. Classes were small and performance was high according to U.S. standards. Students often had to translate their homework from English to their native language, solve the problem in their language, then translate it back into English to be graded. This practice would often take them two to three hours of study daily.

Al and Connie were not only involved in the school but were also in the community in other ways. Al had the opportunity to write speeches for Indonesian diplomats. This gave him greater insight into Indonesian culture. He also taught business English to members of the stock exchange, government, and business for two years. Through this contact, they learned of some local customs. While visiting with one of the government officials, Al learned about one custom, a government program that would be considered brutal in the United States. Once a year the schools would be closed and the students bussed to various sports stadiums for a public hanging of drug dealers. When asked why they did this, they replied emphatically, "Drug dealers hurt our children. We love our children. We hate drug dealers because they hurt our children." The Thompsons were thankful that children at the international school were exempt from mandatory attendance at this spectacle.

Connie was fascinated with all the factories and made it a point to visit many Indonesian industries. One company melted gold and formed it into bars and beautiful gold jewelry. She also visited a cigarette factory where an assembly line consisting of 3000 women worked in rows cutting, rolling, and packaging cigarettes for shipment overseas. Each cigarette had a piece of fresh clove put into it to enhance the smell and for its narcotic effect. Within a couple of hours almost all these women had numb fingers and faces from handling all these cloves.

Alaska and Indonesia managed to cross paths through the clay trumpet cups that got their start with the student corporation in Wainwright. Al had 42,000 clay trumpet cups made by a businessman who owned a large ceramics factory in Indonesia. His 2000 female employees constructed, fired and packaged them on his assembly line. The cups were shipped to Los Angeles where they were then distributed to zoos, museums and aquariums throughout the United States.

Because both Al and Connie loved scuba diving, Indonesia was paradise! They often went to Borneo to explore this area's ocean flora and fauna. During one remarkable 90-foot dive, Al was able to photograph Connie in front of a World War II Japanese battleship that had been sunk by a torpedo. Because the ship blew apart, they were able to swim through its various compartments, exploring its many components.

While hiking in the backcountry of Borneo, they came upon a Japanese artillery site where there were numerous empty artillery shells scattered about. They kept one as a collector's item, adding to an ever-growing menagerie of interesting historic memorabilia.

They attended a funeral where the deceased was burned on a funeral pyre, the body placed on a large stack of wood. They witnessed this for two hours, the pyre burning the whole time and even after they left.

They became quite familiar with the leper colony compound that was less than a mile from their house. Leprosy, also known as Hansen's disease, has been a fully-curable disease since the 1940s, and in 2016 an effective vaccine was introduced. But in Surabaya in the 1990s, it was still a feared infectious bacterial disease that caused skin lesions and numbness in a person's extremities. The disease also carried with it a social stigma that discouraged healthy people from associating with the victims of leprosy. These lepers in Indonesia were isolated by a very strict government mandate and had no access to the care that they needed for a cure. They were consigned to spending their lives in the leper colony, separated from the community and forgotten by most.

Al and Connie toured the colony on a field trip with their students. They witnessed how thin and emaciated the lepers were and sensed the loneliness and despair that lived there with them. They saw one beautiful woman who was not affected by the disease who told them she chose to live there with her husband who was afflicted with the disease. It would only be a matter of time before she also contracted the disease.

Normally the residents had soup day after day, prepared in a 55-gallon drum, cooked over an open fire, in the colony "kitchen". Obviously, this was not enough to provide proper nourishment for the 175 or more residents of the colony. Al, Connie and the students wanted to help, and it was suggested that they could buy meals for the residents.

The students were willing to donate their own money to buy a meal for every resident once a month. For only twenty-five cents each, they could provide a box lunch that included meat, rice, a vegetable, and tea to drink. These boxes were passed out personally to each leper, the residents' gratitude visible on their smiling faces when they received this nourishing meal. The Thompsons and their students did this once a month for two years, never considering the risks to themselves. Although no one contracted leprosy, this contact did make an impact on the students in other ways as they saw people with parts of their faces missing or with horrible deformities. The residents saw the students as wonderful people who brought them this nourishing food. They were thankful for the footprints that brought them this gift.

CHAPTER 15

FIELD TRIP: INDONESIA TO THE ARCTIC

While teaching at Surabaya International School in Indonesia, Al was able to give a thorough first-person account of what he saw and learned while living in the Gates of the Arctic National Reserve at Anaktuvuk Pass, Alaska. In addition, he had gained Arctic experience working on the *Sourdough* movie documenting life in the Brooks Range, part of which is inside the boundaries of Gates of the Arctic. These accounts fascinated his students in his biology class so much that in 1993 he took two of them, Matt from the United States and Richard from Australia, on a field trip of epic proportions.

Once they made it to Alaska, their extended field trip began with a chartered float plane flight out of Bettles, Alaska, to a remote lake. After they set up camp for the night, they started on one of their goals–collecting plant life indigenous to the Arctic. Fourteen botanical species were collected, pressed and dried for permanent use in the Surabaya International School's science program: the very light pink Arctic poppy, the Arctic blue primrose, the bearberry and common fireweed, Labrador tea, purple saxifrage, yarrow and more. It took the entire two weeks to locate all these specimens as it required exploring a 35 square-mile area, setting up a new camp every night.

Another major point of interest during this field trip was seeing the Brooks Range, a 700-mile-long mountain chain with 3000' to over 7000' peaks, the world's highest mountain range within the Arctic Circle. These arrigetch (which means "fingers of the hand extended") peaks are largely composed of granite. However, limestone is also found in these mountains and sometimes contains marine fossils, evidence of this area's under-sea-water past. This range is considered to be part of the Rocky Mountain chain that runs north and south in the lower United States, but these mountains are twisted so dramatically by the geological forces of plate tectonics and volcanic activity that instead of running north and south, in Alaska they run east and west. This area bears witness to a truly remarkable geological history that is not found anywhere else on the North American continent.

The Gates of the Arctic National Reserve is an intact ecosystem, with almost no evidence of the 13,000 years of nomadic hunters and gatherers who lived off the land. As such, there are no trails or roads except those that the animal populations have left behind in their movement across the area. Very few human visitors come to the area so that the native wildlife has no experience of interactions with people and, consequently, little fear of humans. One day, the three explorers hiked about 25 miles to a lake that had no name. On this summer day, there was abundant sunshine and they were tired after their long hike. They laid down for a short nap, but after about an hour, Al opened his eyes and was surprised to see an Arctic fox sound asleep not more than 20 feet away from their small group. The warm sun and isolation provided the opportunity for a welcome nap for the fox as well as the humans. Al arose and took two steps, the fox awoke, stared at Al, slowly shook himself and walked off, obviously not afraid of these intruders into his domain.

Another wildlife interaction involved a mother caribou and calf who were feeding on the tundra moss. The humans came over a hill and spotted the pair. The caribou looked up, spotted them and continued eating, unperturbed as the humans continued down the mountain.

The trip was a success and they returned to Surabaya with a beautiful collection of Arctic flowers, an excellent rock collection, and memories that they hold forever. This may have been a factor that encouraged Matt to become a biologist for the fish and wildlife service in Idaho years later.

CHAPTER 16

ROUND ISLAND WALRUSES

In 1993, while they were living in Indonesia, Al went on another trip that has become what he describes as one of the most interesting expeditions he has ever taken—which is saying a lot for this intrepid explorer. This trip was to Round Island (near the bottom edge of the map) one of seven remote islands in Bristol Bay, south of Dillingham, Alaska. This tiny steep-sided rocky island is only about a tenth of a mile wide. About 15,000 Pacific male walruses come here to recuperate after mating season every spring and summer while the females go north to the retreating ice edge to give birth and raise their young. The male walruses haul out onto the rocky beaches, grunting and making "singing" sounds that have an eerie almost metallic sound like a large bell clanging.

Very few people were allowed to visit this island, so Al was fortunate to be able to go with his long-time friend, Jack, who was a member of the U.S. Marine Mammal Commission at the time. Jack was allowed to take two guests with him, so Al and Matt, the student at the Surabaya High School in Indonesia (who also went to the Gates of the Arctic with Al), were included in this Arctic adventure. Jack was on a scientific mission to observe and count the walrus returning from the Bering Sea and Al and Matt were privileged to have this rare opportunity to join him.

Al, Matt and Jack's journey began with a boat ride from Dillingham, Alaska. The island's rock wall, away from where the walrus gathered and where boats could unload their passengers, was so steep and high that one couldn't get onto the island without some ingenious engineering. Their 25-foot skiff was guided over an underwater device that resembled a cradle. The boat, once over the cradle, was lifted up out of the water by a cable that was about fifty feet long and strung across a very small and narrow inlet. A winch on the cable was run by a generator that, when fired up, would haul the boat up and suspend it into the air before it was set onto the steep-sided rocky island where the passengers could then climb out onto the rocks.

Upon their arrival at Round Island, there were about 2,000 walruses sunning themselves on the beach. The men set up camp and prepared to observe the walruses returning to these beaches from the icy water of the Bering Sea. The walruses are forced to the beaches in the spring when the Arctic ice pack recedes.

When the walruses return, these 1700-to-3000-pound animals are almost white, described by Al as an amazing sight. Their color is so pale because they have been immersed in the icy 28-to-30-degree waters of the Bering Sea for an extended period of time, affecting blood flow to their skin. Their color will return to normal in about a week as they warm up and their blood flow returns to their extremities in these shallow warmer waters.

The men spent a week climbing the primitive trails that allowed them to observe walrus behaviors, their coming and going into the feeding grounds. Numerous males would fight to protect their territory, using their tusks (upper canine teeth that grow for their entire lives and can be three feet long) and loudly bellowing voices to warn other males away from their space.

Besides the walruses, the island has an abundant population of murres, puffins, and other sea birds, sea lions, gray whales, orcas, and some humpbacks. In fact, approximately 250,000 sea birds return to Round Island to raise their young on the rocky cliffs. They were able to observe usually docile puffins fighting for space on the steep cliffs to lay their eggs. They also observed fox populations on various parts of the island. Their one-week stay went quickly as they tracked walrus populations, observed all the other abundant wildlife, and performed the necessary camping chores, a week Al will never forget.

CHAPTER 17

HOME IN HOMER 1994-2009

In 1994 the Thompsons moved from Indonesia back to Alaska. They felt their value system was suffering when they saw one of their hired servants helping their young son tie his shoes. They did not feel comfortable raising a child to live this lifestyle and decided it was time to return to Alaska where they would do their own cooking, cleaning... and shoe tying!

Homer is one of the most beautiful cities in Alaska, about 218 miles southwest of Anchorage, on the Kenai Peninsula at the end of the Sterling Highway. One famous feature of Homer is the Homer Spit, a narrow 4.5-mile-long gravel bar that extends into Kachemak Bay. In contrast to the long and brutal winters they had endured in the Arctic, Homer has long and snowy winters, but not the extreme cold. Homer has an excellent high school and sports program making it a great choice for their move back to the Last Frontier.

Shortly after arriving in Homer, Connie came up with the idea of opening a preschool/daycare center. Being a retired first grade and elementary teacher, this transition was natural and easy. She opened Bear Creek Learning Center for children aged zero to twelve years, and it was accredited by the National Association for Family and Child Care. The children loved the Thompson's small zoo of animals: rabbits, chickens, a pygmy goat named Chomper, a cat and a canary. The kids enjoyed all the animals, but especially the goat.

The daycare was built on a hill overlooking Kachemak Bay and Grewingk Glacier. The hill provided sledding in the winter and a nearby stream offered opportunities for the kids to play in the water. Connie operated the daycare center for about twelve years with a population of twelve children. As is typical for this couple, they have kept in touch with some of these children, a great reward after investing so much care for them.

Their son, Michael, enjoyed Homer High School where he set some state swimming records. As a family, they often enjoyed the Bay's wildlife and rain forest. They lived in Homer for 15 years, escaping the cold of the long and dark Alaska winters by snow birding at Chandler, Arizona. It was also during these years in Homer that Al decided Michael needed a lesson in working! Thus was born Icy Bay Seafoods.

A Bit of Switzerland Comes to Homer

Connie, being a member of a large close-knit family, knew what a joy it was to have many siblings. Al remembers when he visited their family for the first time, there were about 14 people who came to sit around the table. It was a severe blow to them both when they found they would not be able to have their own biological children. It was a great blessing to be able to expand their family through adoption. This desire for family also led to the idea that when their youngest son, Michael, was a teenager, he would benefit from having a foreign exchange student in their home. Christophe, a 16-year-old from the French-speaking area of Switzerland known as Valais, was selected to live with them for a year. He and Mike got along well, participating in many of the same sports and attending many of the same classes.

When Christophe arrived in Homer, he could only speak French which presented some serious challenges. But one year later, this young man was totally fluent in English and was teaching some French at Homer High School. His French teacher was so impressed with his French language abilities that about a third of the way into the year, he was asked to present some of the French lessons every week.

Christophe was an asset to the Icy Bay Seafoods Company that Al had started with Michael. The language barrier seemed to evaporate when people came in contact with his friendly personality whether he was working or playing.

The relationship begun with this foreign exchange student has endured for many years with visits back and forth between Switzerland and Alaska. Hosting this foreign exchange student was a great decision for everyone, in essence, adding one more person to their family, and another place to leave footprints!

CHAPTER 18

ICY BAY SEAFOODS 2004-2012

When Michael was in his teens, he was in need of learning how to work, and he was blessed to have a retired teacher dad who had an entrepreneurial spirit. For eight years, he and Al fished, creating the Icy Bay Seafoods Company. Although they lived in Homer, they fished at Anchorage off of Fire Island in Cook Inlet near the mouth of the Susitna River where they owned two set net fishing permits, regulated by Fish and Game. Fishing season lasted from the end of June through the middle of August, the time of year when the salmon were returning to the streams of their birth to spawn. Every summer, Al and Michael would catch and process about 5,000 pounds of sockeye red salmon which made 3,000 pounds of final smoked product.

Their first year in business was a time of learning. It was very helpful when two fishermen with a site next to theirs taught them how to set the nets and harvest the fish. That first summer they caught 8000 pounds of salmon but quickly discovered that the canneries did not pay them much for the fish they caught. The next summer they purposely caught only 4000 pounds of salmon and decided to try to market their catch themselves. This proved to be a wise decision as the profit margin increased even though the amount of catch decreased.

A day of fishing required that two or three people would be in each of their two 26-foot-long aluminum skiffs, powered by 50 horsepower engines. A 210-foot long by six-foot deep fishnet was deployed, stretched out parallel to the shoreline. The nets had floats along the top edge and weights along the bottom edge, and were moved with the fluctuations of the rising and falling tides that could vary as much as 36 feet. They were able to catch fish with the incoming tides when the fish were swimming in from the open ocean, their gills catching on the nets.

Allen and Michael at work on the Ice Bay Seafoods boats.

The migrating salmon would swim close to the shoreline, moving back and forth with the tides while the fishermen hauled the nets through the water. Once the fish were caught, the net would be pulled into the boat and the fish manually untangled from the net, requiring a large amount of muscle power for this physically demanding job. Sometimes the job was further complicated when creatures other than salmon would get caught in the net. For instance, one day a beluga whale was accidentally caught and had to be cut out of the net. The resultant hole took a long time to repair, but the beluga was unharmed.

Because the canneries did not pay them a fair price for the fish they caught, after a couple of years Al put his mind to the challenge and came up with a better idea. He obtained a permit to slaughter their fish immediately after they were caught and while still on their boats. The salmon guts were tossed into the ocean and were washed out to sea where the halibut would feed on this nutritious by-product. The gutted and cleaned fish were stored on ice in a large tub until the boat returned to shore. None of the other 20 set net permit holders had ever thought of processing their fish harvest themselves, but after a few years of seeing Icy Bay Seafoods' success, many other commercial fishermen followed their lead. It was a great idea, but also physically demanding, and resulted in Al needing carpal tunnel surgery after a few years of cleaning thousands of fish.

Once on land, the salmon were smoked by a local smoker business, and some were flown to San Francisco, Los Angeles, and Scottsdale for winter marketing. By this time, Mike had graduated from high school and was able to accompany Al on marketing trips where they would sell close to 3000 pounds of smoked salmon in Scottsdale, Arizona, around the Super Bowl for $32.50 a pound. Advertising their product in the local Los Angeles newspapers helped them to sell large quantities of their fish at a local farmers' market. During the summer, they sold their fish at the Anchorage Market. They paid their taxi drivers with fish in these towns while they delivered their product. Customers everywhere were happy to be able to buy this nutritious Alaska catch!

However, all good things must end. At the end of eight years, it was time to move on to other things. Mike had enjoyed the fishing venture as much as his dad, had learned the value of hard work, and had gone on to use this knowledge as an adult in the business world. They got out of the lucrative fishing business when they sold their permits to a person who owned a restaurant in Anchorage.

University of Alaska at Anchorage heard of the method they used to process and market their catch themselves. Al was hired by the University to teach a three-month class designed for Alaska fishermen on how to market their finished fish products. This has become a strong business in Alaska as well as the "lower 48" where many Alaska fishermen take their product to sell rather than going through the canneries.

CHAPTER 19

AN EXPLOSIVE HOBBY

Al's biggest hobby interest in his 20s, 30s and 40s was exploring volcanoes. He has explored four volcanic areas in depth and visited another, along with Connie, his willing accomplice. As Al says, and as Connie has had ample opportunities to show, "Love conquers all."

Mount Katmai's violent June 6-8, 1912, eruption was the largest eruption by volume in the 20th century, leaving a 2000-foot-deep caldera. The pyroclastic flow raced down the sides of the mountain at more than 100 miles an hour. Ash blew as much as twenty miles into the air and was deposited on the valley floor over an area of 40 square miles, deep enough that it took decades to cool. The explosive rumbling was heard from the valley all the way to Juneau and Fairbanks. Darkness reigned in Alaska for two days and earthquakes continued until mid-August.

On a sunny day in the summer of 1965, Al and Connie decided to undertake the strenuous 13-mile hike from the entrance of the Valley of the Ten Thousand Smokes to the base of the Mount Katmai volcano, an interesting place for Al and Connie to leave some Alaska footprints. The sandy floor of the Valley of the Ten Thousand Smokes is one of the most unstable landforms in the entire state of Alaska, located between the town of King Salmon and Kodiak Island on the Alaska Peninsula (toward the northern end of the Alaska Peninsula). On this day when they visited this valley 53 years after its violent eruption, Al reports that it was still punctuated with live smoking fumaroles, geyser-like plumes of steam rising into the air. Even today, the National Park Service reports that warm steam can be seen rising from the Novarupta dome.

Within minutes of their arrival at the Novarupta Plug on Mount Katmai, an earthquake trembler alerted them to an impending geological event. A nearby volcano erupted and blew a large ash cloud some 10,000 feet into the air. A hot wind blew this ash and smoke toward them forcing them to run for their lives. Al was able to take a couple of quick photos of the on-coming cloud before it overtook them. They started running crossways to the ash-laden cloud and swam Knife Creek to get out of the way of the ash cloud sweeping down the valley floor. Realizing they were fortunate to escape, they went to bed around midnight in their pup tent. They woke up later in an upside-down tent—the strong winds had eroded the sandy soil below the tent and tipped it over. At this point, Al remembers Connie's request after this near disaster, profound in its simplicity: "Can we go home now?" Al was easily convinced so that the next morning, their trek out of the valley began, leaving their footprints behind.

Shortly after their very early start the next morning, a large banana-shaped military helicopter landed close by. Seven men in orange suits jumped out onto the valley floor. To their amazement, Buzz Aldrin and the astronauts training for the 1969 moon landing had arrived! Buzz told them that this environment was ideal for training for the moon landing. It turns out that the surface of the moon is very similar to this valley with the sand and mountains.

Katmai Volcano spewing out an ash cloud.
Photo credit: Allen Thompson

This impressive volcanic event could have been an experience to inspire more volcano explorations, or a discouragement for one not quite so adventurous. For these intrepid explorers, it definitely became an impetus for many more trips into various volcanoes. In fact, Al and Connie have been inside four other famous volcanoes: Italy's Vesuvius, Mexico's Popocatepetl, Indonesia's Mount Bromo, and the Aleutian Peninsula's Aniakchak. They also have visited Hawaii's Mauna Loa.

Indonesia's Mount Bromo is a live volcano and a popular tourist destination. It does not reach great heights, so it is accessible to anyone willing to go on a two-mile donkey ride and then climb a set of steep stairs to the top of the crater. From there, one could look down into the caldera and enjoy an unobstructed view and the strong odor of burning sulfur. While visiting there, Al and Connie witnessed workers, clothed only in loincloths, hiking down into this caldera to cut out blocks of sulfur. Once burdened with this heavy load on their backs, they hiked up inside the caldera, over the edge, down the mountain, and on to sell this sulfur to a match company two miles away.

Popocatepetl, close to Mexico City, erupted many years ago. The flow covered an entire village including the village jail. They were intrigued to see that a large cathedral was surrounded with lava that had oozed into the church, but stopped right at the altar where a statue of Jesus stood.

At Vesuvius, located near Pompeii, Italy, they were able to hike directly inside the volcano where they could see the damage of the most recent March 17, 1944, eruption which occurred during World War II. This volcano was destructive and deadly during the August 79 A.D. eruption that wiped out the Roman village of Pompeii and several other settlements. It is estimated that this eruption killed 2000 people.

Al and Connie visited Aniakchak, near Painter Creek Lodge on the Aleutian Peninsula. The 1935 eruption of Aniakchak created a crater seven miles across. It contains Surprise Lake where the water is extremely hot on the west end, but cool enough on the east end for salmon to spawn.

At Mauna Loa, they drove to the top of the volcano and saw the outer space observatory. They did not climb inside this very important volcano which is actually the world's tallest mountain from sea floor to its peak.

CHAPTER 20

MORE HUNTING TALES FROM THE LAST FRONTIER

One of the things that draws people to Alaska is the abundant wildlife. The fish, whales, orcas, Steller sea lions, puffins, ptarmigans, ravens, bald eagles, Dall sheep, mountain goats, moose, elk, musk ox, caribou, brown and black bears and more are always an awe-inspiring sight out in the wild. Tourists pay lots of their hard-earned money just to see them. One has to always remember that this wild land is *their* home and we are only visitors. They are built to survive in this environment, and we are most certainly not.

And then there are the fishermen and hunters who decide to brave the elements, sometimes far from civilization, sometimes in the harshest of weather. The following stories of a few of the Thompson hunting encounters are an illustration of just what could happen on a hunting trip! And a cautionary tale to illustrate that maybe a hunting license would be a great idea!

Blest Be the Hunt that Binds

In October 1961, Connie, even though by now she must have known Al's adventurous spirit and perhaps that he wasn't the most cautious of men, agreed to go on a caribou hunt with her husband of just a few months.

They didn't know too many people in the Fairbanks area yet, but their good friends, Jan and Jerry, that Connie knew from her college days in Montana, were living in the Fairbanks area. In fact, it was they who encouraged Al and Connie to homestead and helped them every step along the way. Jerry was going caribou hunting with his friends, so Allen thought it might be a good idea if he and Connie also went on their own caribou hunting venture. Off they went to the remote area north of Tok on the Fortymile River.

It wasn't all that difficult to get their caribou—that was the easy part of the story. However, traveling back to Fairbanks with a smelly bloody caribou in the back of their truck with a nice camper shell was not a pleasant experience. The camper did help conceal the caribou that they shot with no hunting license, which was certainly a potential problem!

On their drive back to Fairbanks, a violent blizzard swept in making it almost impossible to see where they were driving. They came upon two people who had gone into the ditch. In this harsh environment, one always stops to help someone in need, so, of course, they picked up the two and squeezed them into their truck.

Conversation started between the four, discussing what their occupations were. They found out that the rescued peoples' names were Mary and Jack, and Jack worked for Fish and Game. This was a conversation killer for the next few miles as the stench of the dead caribou and the fact that they had no hunting license made Al and Connie a bit speechless and more than a bit nervous.

The next question, "Where are you from?" revealed the fact that Jack was from Montana and had attended Montana State in Bozeman where Connie had gone to college. More discussion revealed that he was the brother of a girl who had been best friends with Connie's sister in college. These "small world" coincidences helped start a friendship that endured for many years.

Years later when Al and Connie felt secure in this friendship, they sheepishly told Jack that way back in 1961 when they had the caribou in the back that was smelling up the whole truck, they had no hunting license. Jack laughed and said, "Yeah, I could tell there was a caribou back there!"

Over the years, memories of this day have provided many good laughs compounded by the fact that the Thompsons, with their lack of experience in such things, discovered that caribou bull meat is not edible when it is killed during rut (mating) season. Although Connie tried preparing the meat in every way she knew how, it could not be eaten and had to be thrown away.

It might be that Connie questioned Al's Alaska expertise just a bit after this event.

Caribou and Ancient Hunting Camps

In the early 1960s, Al and his two friends, Don and Dennis, decided on a cold winter day to drive to the Paxson Lake area to go caribou hunting. Traditionally, a large herd of thousands migrated through a pass twenty-eight miles north of Paxson Lake where lies Swede Lake.

After parking their vehicles, they began hiking through the tundra and rolling hills four to five miles to Swede Lake. After many hours and not seeing any caribou, they noticed a hill near the lake that might give them a better chance of seeing caribou. When they summited the hill, they saw a number of caribou and shot two of them.

While the men were dressing them out, they became chilled, so cold that they needed to build a fire to warm up. When they began digging out a place for the fire, they discovered numerous stone chips and a couple of useless misshapen arrow heads left behind when someone, perhaps centuries ago, on this spot had been making arrowheads. This was a mystery they would later enlist help in solving.

After they got their two caribou all dressed out, doused the fire, and while they hiked the four miles back to their vehicle in the growing dark, an intense snow storm blew in. It became very difficult to keep hiking while carrying the heavy caribou on their backs, constantly using the big mountains as a guide to find their vehicle. Exhausted, they finally made it to the road.

They had seen no traffic but when two trucks spotted the hunters, they stopped, picked up the three men and their caribou and took them to their vehicle. At this point, they discovered the two trucks were being driven by Alaska game wardens. It was a very good thing the wardens did not ask the men for their hunting licenses as they had none! The hunters thought maybe the blizzard made travel so difficult that the weather was the topic of conversation the whole drive back to their vehicles.

They arrived at their own vehicles, offloaded the caribou, thanked the game wardens and waited five hours before they headed home. They had to pass a game check station before getting on the main road, so the wait was to avoid having to admit that they had no hunting licenses. The blowing snow, late hours, and darkness helped them avoid this accountability as the station was closed down when they finally drove past it.

Later they reported finding these stone fragments and arrowheads to the University of Alaska at Fairbanks. This led to a full-scale three-year search and exploration of this site and the conclusion that where the three men had been hunting had been an ancient hunting camp dating back as far as 10,000 to 15,000 years ago. Other hunters long before Al, Don, and Dennis had also decided this was a great place to hunt and had camped here season after season, perhaps for many weeks, shaping their arrowheads.

The Mountain Goat Mistake

One winter, Al and his good friend, Jerry, decided to trap wolves and wolverines at Caribou Creek near Sheep Mountain north of Palmer, Alaska. Normally, when trapping, one expects to catch foxes, wolves, and wolverines, but not a 600-pound mountain goat. On this day, they set traps in a narrow gulch between two steep mountains. Traditionally, traps were set and any animal caught was slaughtered on the spot. This would not be a normal day, though.

A full-grown mountain goat, all 600 pounds of him, was caught by its hind legs in a #4 trap designed to catch much smaller animals. They were shocked and surprised by this catch. They didn't know what to do on this mid-February day when they inadvertently trapped this animal out of season. To slaughter this animal would be a violation of hunting law.

They, in good conscience, could not leave the goat in this predicament but that put them in a difficult situation of explaining to Fish and Game that they did not intend to trap this goat. They decided to kill the goat, load it onto a sled pulled by a snow machine over frozen Caribou Creek, take it to Fish and Game, explain the situation, and hope they would not be arrested for illegally harvesting the goat out of season.

Halfway down the creek on his snow machine, with the goat pulled behind on his sled, Jerry crossed a patch of thin ice. Immediately, they broke through the ice and went down into the icy waters of the creek. Jerry fell forward and was able to hold onto the icy edge while Al pulled him up out of the water. The snow machine was wedged under the ice between a gravel bar and the ice. Meanwhile, the sled with the goat twisted in the current, broke loose from the snow machine, and went down the river under the ice. The men could hear the goat and sled bumping and crashing under the ice, traveling all the way to the Matanuska River, and there was nothing they could do about it. The goat and sled, as well as the snow machine, were never seen again, likely wedged beneath the ice by rocks.

They reported the incident to Fish and Game in Anchorage, just to keep it legal. The game warden was stunned by their story. Al and Jerry showed them the trap with the blood and goat hair on it. The officials concluded it was, indeed, a freak accident, and a hunting violation would not be charged against them. The game warden said he had never heard of such an unusual event.

The Bear

Al and his friend Dennis were scoping out bears on Swede Mountain near Swede Lake, Alaska. On this particular gorgeous fall day, there were five large grizzly bears feeding on blueberries. After some time, they decided to stalk one of the bears and positioned themselves within shooting range. After getting into position, a bear was spotted 400 yards away. Al was to shoot first, and if he missed, Dennis was to fire.

Al lined up the bear in his sights, pulled the trigger but nothing happened–a misfire! The gun was jammed! Dennis fired, hit the bear, and it took off into the brush. Another bear was frightened by the shot and ran about a hundred feet right in front of them up the mountain so close that they could hear its heavy breathing. It was fortunate that the second bear didn't see them! With that danger past, the immediate problem was a wounded bear with only one rifle to finish him off since Al's rifle was not working.

As they followed the tracks up the mountain, they could see the bear was seriously wounded. After an hour of tracking him, it was too dark and dangerous to continue the pursuit. They decided to go back to the cabin and contact John, a local trapper, who had a remarkable tracking dog. That dog had over 150 stitches in him from previous encounters with wild animals and could ride right behind the snow machine for six to eight hours. He was quite the dog!

John and the dog rode up the mountain the next day and tracked the bear. Within a day, the dog found the bear which was then killed. Its wounds would have prevented it from surviving the winter.

Stray Bullets and Miracles

Allen was hunting moose with his friends Roy and Norm
in the remote mining area of Petersville, Alaska, traveling
in a large snow track vehicle that could carry six people.
They had forded the Petersville River in water so deep that
the vehicle almost stalled. When they got to flat land, they
lifted the hood of the vehicle to drain the carburetor when
suddenly Al felt a terrible pain in his right hand just before
hearing a rifle shot. Immediately, his hand swelled and
started bleeding. At nearly the same moment, Norm fell to
the ground clutching his profusely bleeding thigh.

Because Norm had been bent over working on the carburetor,
he had narrowly missed being hit in the back of his head
by the stray bullet that had ricocheted off the hood, pierced
Al's hand, and then entered Norm's leg.

To add to the suspense, a large moose came running toward
them, the victim for which the bullet was intended. That
bullet didn't stop the moose, but the next one, fired by Roy
who had been sitting atop the vehicle, did. The moose fell,
and a man came out of the woods holding a rifle. When the
man realized what his bullet had done, he was astounded
that the bullet could have passed through the woods and
traveled the distance across the flat land to injure these two
men leaving the moose unscathed.

A tourniquet was applied to Norm's leg, Al's hand was
bandaged, and then Roy tended to the really important
business of dressing out the moose. After that was done,

then, and only then, did they once again ford the river and head to Anchorage and the emergency room at the hospital. There the bullet was removed from Norm's leg. Even though there was no bullet in Al's hand, he did have seven metal fragments embedded in it, shrapnel from the hood of the vehicle. It was determined that these fragments should be left alone because of the nerve damage that would be caused by trying to remove them.

Years later Al had carpal tunnel surgery and the x-rays showed that those souvenir fragments were still firmly in place, a reminder of how a bullet could be a part of a miracle.

CHAPTER 21

THE THOMPSON LEGACY

Besides his strong leadership with the Native Corporations that had made an impact on Native students while they lived in Wainwright, Al was pleased to realize he had a remarkable career and influence on many children who attended school in Anchorage as well. A significant project was inspired by his position as a work study coordinator for the handicapped students in the Anchorage schools. The program started because of his interest in students who were failing in school. He realized the value of making practical classes available for students as early as their freshmen year, focusing on life skills. These students were enrolled in classes for success in daily survival such as managing money, shopping for food and clothing, and raising a family.

Al's Master's degree from the University of Alaska at Fairbanks dealt specifically with the academic and work skills needs of handicapped students. He used this education to begin a three-year experiment at West Anchorage High School where work skills, learning about types of jobs, how to get along at a job, and learning about the skills that are needed to hold a job, were taught. The three-year experiment is now a program that has been in operation for 30 years and is well known throughout the Anchorage School District.

Years later, Jerry Straus, a counselor and friend, approached Al and wanted to know more about this work study program. Jerry knew of many students who dropped out of school, went to work, and could not be promoted because they lacked a high school diploma. Al worked with Jerry full time for four years to get the new SAVE (Specialized Academic Vocational Education) program launched, patterned after the work study program. This allows a student who dropped out of school to re-enroll, work full time and attend night school to complete his or her high school diploma. As of today, there are approximately 800 students attending the SAVE program in the Anchorage School District.

Recently as an Anchorage Lion's Club member, Al was making a presentation to the Anchorage District School Board. After completing his talk, a member of the audience stood up, was recognized by the Board president and spoke to the audience. He told the audience that Al was his counselor in the work study program in the early 2000s. He is now a successful painting contractor in the Anchorage area. Al was stunned when the audience arose and gave him a standing ovation for the success of the program. Of all the good things that ever happened to Al, he will never forget this expression of appreciation.

Allen's Parting Footprints

It is hard to imagine these two not being right in the middle of many projects and adventures, but as happens to us all if we are blessed to live long enough, when this couple reached their 80s, they did at least slow down—a bit—still walking side by side, leaving important footprints on their family, friends, and community.

Reflecting back over the years, Al would tell you that he has learned many things during his 80 plus years of life, accepting the challenges placed before him and even seeking out others, leaving footprints in some unexpected places. First, he acknowledges that God has given him the wonderful gift of life. He was blessed to be adopted at an early age by a loving and stable family. Growing up in rural Montana with parents who believed in teaching their children the value of hard work sent him off with a set of skills and values necessary for the life God set before him. He understood the blessing it was to have the opportunity to get a college education and become a teacher, substitute teaching yet into his 80s. And on top of all that, he was blessed to marry a remarkable woman who shared his love of teaching and travel and joined him in countless ventures.

His many close calls and near-death experiences affirm Al's strong belief that God had plans for him, expecting him to make good use of his second and third chances to accomplish more in his life. His desire to teach gave him the avenue through which he was able to influence his students, changing the direction of the footprints of many young people who otherwise would have been faced with failure in our society.

Connie's Parting Footprints

Reflecting back over the years, Connie remembers what it was like, a naive Montana farm girl, moving to Alaska and assuming they would make money, buy a house, raise good Christian children, and live happily ever after. She soon found out that her intelligent, ambitious, and curious husband would lead her through many rewarding and challenging years.

Connie learned to expect sometimes sudden, unexpected, and not always welcome changes. She learned to accept the changes, even if not always agreeing with them. Some of these changes were good and she grew through them. Some were difficult, making life sometimes feel like an out-of-control roller coaster ride. She felt she was not a strong person or that her voice counted for much. While growing up as the fifth of eight siblings, she learned that her voice seldom counted and did not feel like that had changed when she was a married adult.

Challenges were all around them from their decision to homestead as newlyweds to moving back to Anchorage and "civilization." For most of their marriage they were seldom in one place for many years in a row, pursuing Allen's almost endless quest to try something new. The heartbreak of the loss of their earthly possessions not only once, but three times, served to show both Connie and Al what was truly valuable to them—their family and the opportunity to use their gift of teaching. Through it all, they were surrounded by the love and support of family and friends. These are the things that brought them true joy.

As one would expect, Connie did not just sit back and let the world pass her by as a senior citizen. When in her 80s, it was obvious that one of their granddaughters was having great difficulty learning to read, and she was already in fifth grade. This reading challenge would soon impact all her learning. She was not making much progress even though she was placed into special education classes.

Connie was well versed in the EnListen program which uses classical music to stimulate the growth of the brain. Within two years of completing the program, their granddaughter was placed into the gifted reading program at the elementary school. This achievement was accomplished by Connie's persistent use of the EnListen program and special tutors. By the time this granddaughter reached her high school years, she loved to read and did well in all her subjects. This program and a dedicated teacher/grandma changed her prospects and the trajectory of her footprints.

Footprints, Walking Side by Side

When the Thompsons arrived in Alaska in the 1960s, almost everyone was a "transplant," not born and raised there. Their friends, many of them teachers, became their family and sometimes even business partners. They camped together, shared meals, and celebrated birthdays. The men hunted together. Even though after retirement they lived in three different states, they tried to get together as often as possible.

The two of them agree that another life-long blessing came into their lives with the adoption of their three children. Throughout the years these three have given back the gifts of happiness and love. They are thankful for the six grandchildren that have enriched their lives beyond words.

The development of Al's faith in God was strongly influenced by the Christian witness and influence of Connie. In his own words, he says, "I am humbled by the gift of happiness that God has bestowed on me." Connie had always admired his energy and willingness to do whatever needed to be done, always friendly and willing to talk to anyone. And all this he did with a kind and generous spirit. They are truly a couple that God has put together and used for His good purpose.

Allen and Connie

Al and Connie were blessed to renew their wedding vows at their son's wedding which just happened to be on their 60th wedding anniversary, July 22, 2021, celebrating so many years of leaving footprints side by side. That momentous day they were given the gift of a second daughter-in-law. What a long way they had come since the celebration of their first anniversary when they were stranded at that Fairbanks homestead with no way to go anywhere to celebrate.

As is likely true for every human who has walked this planet, there is a desire to leave a mark—a footprint—of some significance that will remain after they are gone. With the influence they have left behind through their teaching careers, it is likely that the Thompsons have succeeded in leaving lasting footprints in the Last Frontier. And one does not have to look all that closely to see that third set of footprints that belongs to their loving and gracious God who was holding their hands and walking with them every step of the way.

Printed in the United States
by Baker & Taylor Publisher Services